Choice Notes on the PSALMS

F.B. Meyer Memorial Library

Devotional Commentary on Exodus
Choice Notes on Joshua to 2 Kings
Choice Notes on the Psalms
Devotional Commentary on Philippians

Choice Notes on the PSALMS

by
F.B. Meyer

Foreword by
J. Arnold Fair

KREGEL PUBLICATIONS
Grand Rapids, Michigan 49501

Library of Congress Cataloging-in-Publication Data

Meyer, F.B. (Frederick Brotherton), 1847-1929.
Choice Notes on the Psalms.

Reprint. Originally published: The Psalms. London: Morgan & Scott.
1. Bible. O.T. Psalms—Criticism, interpretation, etc. I. Title.
BS1430.M49 1984 223.'206 84-17109
ISBN 0-8254-3242-1

2 3 4 5 6 Printing/Year 91 90 89 88 87

Printed in the United States of America

CONTENTS

Contents

FOREWORD

"Blessed is the man that walketh not in the counsel of the ungodly, nor standeth in the way of sinners, nor sitteth in the seat of the scornful." So opens the magnificent, majestic book of Psalms. The book closes with the words, "Let every thing that hath breath praise the Lord. Praise ye the Lord." Between these two verses is a mountain range of supernal peaks and pleasant placid valleys of spiritual discernment and refreshment. It is the daily reading and study of the Psalms that will lead one to walk in the holiness of God.

Choice Notes on the Psalms by F. B. Meyer is a classic in its brevity and beauty of clarity. As you begin to read the plain pithy remarks, it is as though you were entering the halls of a very special sacred school. Here is a valued volume that will give delight and blessed learning.

F. B. Meyer is an excellent teacher. As you study many of these Psalms you will sense you are in the classroom of divinely prepared instruction. The teaching is not only delightfully devotional, it is pointedly practical. The precepts and principles are as fresh as this day and as useful as one's breath. Being a scholar of the inspired Word of God, Dr. Meyer is convinced here is truth presented not to be merely considered but to be regularly used with alertness in the active arena of life.

As one proceeds through the schooling of these chapters, one realizes that he has entered some chapters that are laboratory rooms in the life of David and observes the vital experiments of life that have been carried out and expressed. As an astute instructor, F.B. Meyer is quick to point out the formula for righteous success and the dangers which lead to destruction. Here he rejoices over the results of triumph and laments the tragedies which can be viewed.

Though there are many lessons to be learned—this is Psalms—and one is conscious he is never far from the music department.

Here are the chapters where one can hear the great crescendos of praise. It is here that the glorious melodies break forth with the expressions: "Bless the Lord, O my soul" and "Praise ye the Lord." And yet as we make our way through other Psalms of contrite confession, we are conscious of a lonely, luting lyric. Though weeping may endure for a night, Dr. Meyer presents the soothing harmonies of comfort in an applicable manner.

Dr. F. B. Meyer is pastorally at his best in this brief commentary. Wise will be the person who learns to glean well where this disciplined pastor walked with God. Your life will be enriched. It is an honor and joy to commend this volume.

J. Arnold Fair

INTRODUCTION

THE Jewish Psalms have furnished the bridal hymns, the battle songs, the pilgrim marches, the penitential prayers, and the public praises of every nation in Christendom, since Christendom was born. "They have rolled through the din of every great European battlefield; they have pealed through the scream of the storm in every ocean highway of the world. Drake's sailors sang them when they clave the virgin waters of the Pacific; Frobisher's, when they dashed against the barriers of Arctic ice and night. They floated over the waters on that day of days when England held her freedom against Pope and Spaniard, and won the naval supremacy of the world. They crossed the ocean with the *Mayflower* pilgrims; were sung round Cromwell's camp fires, and his Ironsides charged to their music; whilst they have filled the peaceful homes of England with the voice of supplication and the breath of praise. In palace halls, by happy hearths, in squalid rooms, in pauper wards, in prison cells, in crowded sanctuaries, in lonely wilderness—everywhere they have uttered our moan of contrition and our song of triumph; our tearful complaints, and our wrestling, conquering, prayer."*

About one-third of the Psalms are anonymous. Seventy-three bear the name of David, "the sweet Psalmist of Israel." Twenty-four are attributed to the minstrels of his reign, and to subsequent singers; some of whom may have lived in the glorious period of Ezra's restoration. Two are attributed to Solomon; and one to Moses, "the man of God."

The inscriptions of the Psalms have given rise to much discussion. Some of them indicate the musical accompaniment, which had been carefully selected—whether with flutes, as the 5th; or with stringed instruments, as the 6th. Others express

* Rev. Baldwin Brown.

the intentions of the Psalms—to TEACH; to BRING TO REMEMBRANCE; to GIVE THANKS. Others again commemorate the circumstances under which the Psalms they head were penned; as for instance the 56th, which is entitled, "The silent dove in far-off lands," and commemorates the time when David was an exile in the land of the Philistines.

The Hebrew Title for this precious collection of Sacred Hymns is PRAISES; and rightly so, for the most prominent feature in them is *Praise.* The rendering of this word into Greek gives us our title PSALMS.

There are FIVE BOOKS embraced in this collection:—

THE FIRST, including 1-41; ending with the doxology and a double Amen.

THE SECOND, including 42-72; ending in the same way, and with the further addition that: "The prayers of David, the son of Jesse, are ended."

THE THIRD, including 73-89; ending with a somewhat different doxology and a double Amen.

THE FOURTH, including 90-106; ending with doxology, amen, and hallelujah.

THE FIFTH, including 107-150; ending with repeated hallelujahs.

There are three ways in which the Psalms may be studied. We may look at them, first, as recording the inner heart-history of those who wrote them, and especially of David. We cannot understand his life merely by reading the historical books; but when we compare the outer with the inner, and listen to his own musings on the varied episodes of his changeful career, we are able to form an altogether new and realistic conception of that rich and many-chorded nature. It was good that he should be afflicted: that he should extract from the wine-press of his sorrows a cordial to cheer all weary and aching hearts till time shall be no more.

Next, we should study the Psalter in its bearing on our blessed Lord. He said Himself, "It is written in the Psalms concerning Me" (Luke 24:44) ; and He expressed some of his deepest emotions in words borrowed from that marvellous vocabulary. There are some Psalms that are entirely Messianic, for they can have no useful reference but to the Lord Jesus; others have a primary reference to some figure or event in Hebrew story, from which, however, they soon pass on, to find a richer and wider fulfilment in Him to whose person and work all the rays of Scripture converge. It is the Spirit of Christ which breathes throughout the Psalter; and we cannot be surprised if it often rises into tones and expressions of thought which may be uttered by human lips, but certainly emanate from a higher than mortal source. In this sense David's Son is also David's Root.

Lastly, we may study the Psalms *for ourselves*, nourishing our spirits with their rich expressions of experimental religion. Few men have reached such heights of joy, or touched such depths of penitential grief, as David. Nor is there a note in the entire *gamut* of the experiences of the religious life, which does not speak beneath his marvellous touch. When language fails us, these Psalms will often express our deepest selves; our yearnings for God; our contrition for sin; our inexpressible joy. They are like some marble staircase, trodden by myriads of feet, yet unworn and clear-cut still, up which we too may pass from the blessedness of the initial verse, to the ringing hallelujahs that peal out their inspired anthems in the closing sentence of this Golden Book of the inner life.

May He, who is expressly said to have been their Author (II Sam. 23:2; Acts 1:16; 4:25; Heb. 3:7, 8), give us his own divine and blessed help as we seek to open up their sacred and blessed treasures!

Psalm 1 "BLESSED IS THE MAN!"

This Psalm, like a sign-post, points the way to blessedness. The opening word may be read, "Oh, the blessedness!" In this exclamation is embodied the experience of a life, ratified and sealed by the Holy Spirit. The Psalter begins with the same message as the Sermon on the Mount. Religious life is the blessed life; and blessedness is more than happiness. Beneath the lintel of this benediction we pass into the temple of praise.

BLESSEDNESS IS TO BE OBTAINED IN TWO WAYS.—(I) NEGATIVELY.—Avoid the company of the irreligious. (1) You must mix with them in daily business; but do not choose their society. When let go from necessary engagements, make for the people of God (Acts 4:23).

(II) POSITIVELY.—We cannot live on negations; and if we withdraw ourselves from the society of evil men, we must enter the circle of prophets and kings, psalmists and historians, who are ever waiting to greet us with their holiest, noblest thoughts, within the circle of sacred Scripture.

2. It is not enough to read the Bible as a duty—we must come to it with *delight.* And this is possible on these conditions: give yourself up to it; eschew light and foolish literature, which cloys the appetite; ever open the Book in happy felowship with its Author. Nor is it enough to read it cursorily and forget it: we must *meditate,* until, by the process of spiritual digestion, it is assimilated (Jas. 1:25). Better one verse really masticated than a whole chapter bolted.

THE REWARDS OF THE BLESSED MAN (3).— He shall be under Divine culture, *planted* (Ps. 92:13); within reach of perennial supplies, *planted by rivers* (John 7:38, 39); prepared against any demand or emergency—*fruit in season;* unfading beauty and freshness, a spiritual evergreen; and prosperity even in this world, because his life is ordered by discretion and obedience to Divine principles. Joseph realized this picture (Gen. 39:3, 4).

THE CONTRAST TO THE BLESSED MAN (4).—It might be rendered, *Not so the ungodly, not so.* As to their career, all that has been said of the righteous is to be reversed. They go from bad to worse in their choice of company; beginning with the ungodly, and ending with the scornful; and from walking, they pass to standing and sitting, which give the idea of permanence and of settled enjoyment. As to their nature, they are as chaff, which is like wheat, and yet utterly worthless. As to their doom, they shall be forgotten on earth, leaving no trace, taking no root; and in the other world they shall be forever excluded from the festal hosts of the redeemed (Matt. 13:30; Rev. 21:27).

THE COMFORTS OF THE BLESSED MAN.—God knows his way, though dark and difficult. Nothing is hidden from Him who bottles our tears (Ps. 56:8); and He will not let us be over-pressed. And, though the ungodly may appear to prosper at the expense of the righteous, it shall be only for a moment: ultimately the way of the ungodly *shall perish* (*see* Ps. 37). Wherefore, rest in the Lord. Your blessedness is better than the ill-gotten gains of the ungodly, and will last longer.

Psalm 2 "THOU ART MY SON!"

This is one of the sublimest of the Psalms. Its mould is highly dramatic. Attempts have been made to connect it with David or Solomon; but its scope is too vast and majestic to be limited to any earthly monarch. The Psalm can only find its complete fulfillment in Him to whom its glowing passages are referred in Acts 4:25; 13:33; Heb. 1:5; 5:5; Rev. 2:27. A natural division is suggested by the structure of the Psalm into four stanzas of three verses each.

THE DETERMINED HATE OF THE PEOPLE (1-3).—The word *rage* has the idea of the tumultuous concourse of vast crowds of people, swarming with Oriental gesticulations and cries into a central meeting-place, aroused to a frenzy of excitement. *Imagine* is the same word translated *meditate* (1:2); whilst the godly meditates on God's law, the ungodly meditates a project which is *vain*, and shall come utterly to nought. Pilate and Herod and the Jewish rulers are for once at peace among themselves in their common hostility to the Messiah (Luke 23:12, 13). Let us not effect worldly alliances, for the drift of the great ones of the earth is against our Lord. *Compare* verse 3 with Hos. 11:4 and Matt. 11:30.

THE DIVINE TRANQUILITY (4-6).—The scene shifts to heaven; there God is depicted as undismayed—a strong man laughs at the ineffectual efforts of tiny children to throw him down. *Yet I have set,* i.e., *anointed.*—"Messiah" and "Christ" alike mean *anointed.* Our Lord was anointed with the Holy Ghost (Isa. 11: 2, 3; 61:1; Acts 10:38; Luke 4:18; John 3:34). He is God's own King; MY *King;* as Solomon was David's (I Kings 1:37, 38, etc.).

MESSIAH'S MANIFESTO (7-9).—Standing forth, He produces and recites one of the eternal decrees. Before time was, He was the only-begotten of the Father (John 17:5): but his sonship was declared at his Resurrection; then He was born first from among the dead and sealed (Acts 13:30-37; Rom. 1:4; Col. 1:18). The world is his heritage; but the gift is conditional on prayer. For this He pleads through the ages; and, if we are truly at one with Him, we too shall *ask.* The pastoral staff for the sheep; the "iron rod" for those who oppose.

OVERTURES AND COUNSELS OF PEACE (12).—*Kiss,* the expression of homage (I Sam. 10:1). The word "adore" is literally *to the mouth.* To "perish in the way" reminds of 1:6. Notice the change in R.V.; "his wrath will soon be kindled" (Jas. 5:9; Rev. 6:17). *Oh the blessedness!* closes this Psalm as it began the first.

Psalm 3 "I WILL NOT BE AFRAID!"

AN ENUMERATION OF TROUBLE (1, 2).—Though God knows all, it relieves the over-charged heart to make a full statement of anxieties and troubles. The foes were *many.* They quoted his sin as a reason for supposing that God had withdrawn his aid (II Sam. 16:7, 8). The word *help* is *salvation;* but salvation belongeth unto God (8; 35:3).

AN EXPRESSION OF UNFALTERING TRUST (3, 4).—God our shield (Gen. 15:1) is *for i.e., around us.* Would that we found our *glory* in Him only (Jer. 9:23, 24). It is a good thing to use the voice in prayer, as our Lord did. Words keep the heart awake

(Heb. 5:7). David looked to God as dwelling between the cherubim of the ark, the symbol of propitiation; and he thus approached Him, as sinners must ever do, through the Lamb of God, the Priest of man.

An Acknowledgment of Mercy (5, 6).—It was the perfection of trust to be able to sleep under such circumstances, and to be devoid of fear when environed by such mighty hosts. But it is gloriously possible. So Jesus slept (Mark 4:38), and Peter (Acts 12:6). Let us be sure that we are where God would have us to be: then let us resign ourselves to his care; and, even though pursued by the results of our own mistakes and sins, we shall find that He will save us in them, if not from them.

An Urgent Entreaty (7, 8).—For the third time the idea of *salvation* is introduced. The writer's foes are looked upon as wild beasts, who, when their jawbone is broken and their teeth dashed out, may roam around, but are powerless to hurt. David speaks as if he felt that this work were already done, and his foes' rage futile. And he turns from them to the great mass of his people, led wrong by wily conspirators, and pleads that God's best blessings may rest on them. So does our Lord intercede for us.

Psalm 4 "HEAR ME WHEN I CALL!"

A Prayer (1).—We must be sure that our cause is a righteous one before we can ask God to vindicate it; and we do well to go back to God's deliverances from former straits. Build supplication on recollection.

An Expostulation (2, 3).—*Vanity* refers back to 2:1—"a vain thing"; *leasing* is Old English for *lying*. Absalom's rebellion is a type of all those plots against Christ and His saints which begin in falsehood, and end in confusion. The Hebrew word translated *godly* means one who loves. Dost thou love God first, and afterwards His saints? Then know that God hath set thee apart (*i.e.*, separated) for Himself. Seek his praise alone. Be content to let the world go by. Thou canst not fail; his cause and thine are one (Lam. 3:58).

LOVING COUNSEL (4, 5).—The Apostle gives a very remarkable application of verse 4 in Eph. 4:26. If men communed with each other less, and with God and their own heart more, allowing the heat of passion to cool in the silences of the night, they would discover the futility of fuming and fretting against the Lord's people and cause. To all of us the injunction, *Be still*, is most appropriate. It is only in standing water that silt settles, and in quiet nights that the dew distils. In the night, when the eye is closed to all the world besides, let it be opened to self-examination. *Sacrifice* here is the whole burnt offering, and corresponds to entire surrender, out of which *trust* naturally springs.

A WISE DEDUCTION AND RESOLVE (6-8).—How true is this of the "many" everywhere who know not God!—But all is vain when God's face is hidden. How rich is the soul on which its light rests! (Num. 6:24-26). Absalom, and his conspirators, with all that David had left them, had not as much true bliss as the fugitive monarch enjoyed. In the hour of his sin he had asked to hear joy and gladness (Ps. 51:8); and this was the reply. The saint has no need to envy the prosperous worldling (John 4:13,14). May the Holy Spirit "put gladness in our hearts" to-day (Gal. 5:22). *Both*, verse 8, means, "I shall go to sleep as soon as I lie down." God alone is enough for any soul. He suffices for heaven: why not for earth? In our solitude, let us turn to make all in all of Him (Ezek. 34:25).

Psalm 5 "IN THE MORNING"

THE ADDRESS AND MANNER OF PRAYER (1-3).—Uttered *words* are inadequate to convey the deep thought which *meditates*. This latter word will stand for the groanings which cannot be uttered, but which the Spirit understands (Rom. 8:26, 27). Distinguished from either of these, there is urgent ejaculation for aid, described as *the voice of a cry*. As soon as we awake at early dawn, let us speak to God. Let Him be the first to hear our voice. And let us *direct, i.e.*, set in order, our prayer. The same Hebrew word is used in Gen. 22:9; Lev. 1:7; 24:8. We are not to pray without method (Eccles. 5:1). And, having prayed, we must look out for the answer (Hab. 2:1). We miss many answers, because we get tired of waiting on the quays for the returning ships.

Contrasted Characters (4-7).—There are here seven expressions for the ungodly. Evil may not even *sojourn* as a wayfaring man (II John 10). *Leasing* is Old English for *lying.* Not in the spirit of boasting, but of humble gratitude, does David turn to himself (I Cor. 15:10). The Jew in prayer looked towards the temple (Dan. 6:10). The tabernacle was spoken of as Jehovah's temple (I Sam. 1:9; 3:3); so that David may have written these words as they stand, or they may have been revised by Ezra.

The Prayer (8-12).—We may appeal to God's righteousness to vindicate his righteous ones. Because He is what He is, we may count on Him (II Chron. 16:9). The 8th verse is thus parallel to the 4th. This terrible description of the ungodly is almost entirely concerned with the sins of the tongue. It is largely quoted in Rom. 3. Wicked men are like sepulchres, which look fair without, but are full of corruption within and exhale pestilential exhalations. And as by their words they sin against God and mislead the righteous, so by their words they shall be condemned and fall. David here, as God's mouthpiece, pronounces their inevitable doom.

Here again (11) we meet the oft-repeated word, *trust.* And with trust goes joy, as brother and twin sister; and with both goes love. How happy their lot—defended, blessed, and encompassed with the Divine favor! (Deut. 33:23).

Psalm 6 "THE LORD HATH HEARD!"

The first of the Penitential Psalms; the other six being 32, 38, 51, 102, 130, 143. *Sheminith* is evidently a musical term, signifying the octave. The earlier verses of this Psalm are a wail; but it ends in a song. It is like a day of rain which clears at evening. The Psalm is full of beautiful ejaculatory cries.

The Elements of the Psalmist's Sorrow (1-7).—There was the pressure of Divine displeasure on account of sin (1, 2), combined with soul-anguish (3, 4), perhaps accompanied with sickness, bringing nigh unto death (4, 5), whilst enemies (6, 7). In verse 5 David considers the grave as disa[illegible] that active service of praise which is the peculiar pri[illegible] living (Isa. 38:19). He clearly foresaw the Resurrectio[illegible] haps not so clearly the state of the departed, which i[illegible] [illegible]ught to light in the Gospel. How touching is the plea, so suitable for sufferers!—*for I am weak.* How expressive the broken sentence, *How long?* which was often on Calvin's lips! And that prayer, *O Lord, heal me!* may well be on our lips continually.

THE CERTAINTY OF THE PSALMIST'S DELIVERENCE (8-10).—The prayer is no sooner uttered than answered. The consciousness of having been heard steals over the weary soul like a glint of light on to a bed in the hospital ward. David knows that the petition is granted, though it has not yet come to hand (I John 5:15). *Weeping* has a voice for the ear of God. He can interpret sighs and tears (8). In the Revised Version, which we do well to compare with the authorized, the words of verse 10, which read like an imprecation, stand in the future tense—they *shall* be ashamed and turn back. When God returns (4), our enemies turn back (10).

Psalm 7 "IN THEE DO I PUT MY TRUST!"

Shiggaion is thought by some to refer to the erratic and irregular metre. The expressions of this Psalm should be carefully compared with the narrative of events in I Sam. 24; 25; 26. *Cush* may be a covert allusion to Saul, who was a Benjamite. Or it may refer to some "black-visaged" member of his tribe, who was one of David's chief calumniators.

PRAYER (1, 2).—If David desired deliverance from his foes, how much more do we need deliverance from our arch-enemy! (I Pet. 5:8, 9).

PROTESTATION (3-5).—So far from being guilty of the offence charged on him, David, on two occasions, spared Saul's life (I Sam. 24; 26). *Mine honor* is probably only another name for the soul (Gen. 49:6).

AN APPEAL (6-9).—By a bold metaphor, he attributes the

success of his foes to some temporary abdication on God's part of his throne, and entreats Him to reassume his throne, and give his decisions, as Eastern judges are wont to do, in the midst of the people standing around. When we do right and suffer for it, we have a strong argument with God; we standing still, keeping silence, and leaving Him to vindicate (I Pet. 2:20-23). What a noble prayer is verse 9!

PREDICTION (10-16).—Evil recoils like a boomerang on those who set it in motion. Ralph the Rover perished at the Inchcape Rock. The huntsman at eventide falls into the pit prepared in the morning for his prey, covered by the branches and reeds and earth.

Psalm 8 "HOW EXCELLENT IS THY NAME!"

Was *Gittith* a tune or instrument brought from Gath? (I Sam. 27:2). This exquisite ode, which can only reach its fulfilment in the person of the Son of Man—to whom it is referred in the New Testament (Heb. 2:6-9)—was evidently composed at night. It probably dates from the early shepherd days, when wild creatures crept around the fold, and night-birds screamed, reminding the sweet singer of the animal world, as constituting the human kingdom.

THE INSCRIPTION (1).—Jehovah our Lord (*Adonai*) (*see* Ps. 110:1. Our Lord Jesus is here.

THE ASCRIPTION (1-2).—His name excellent on earth; his glory the crown on the brow of the sky. And so mighty that his strength communicated to babes is more than enough to vanquish and silence His foes (I Cor. 1:25). See also Christ's own quotation (Matt. 21:16). Oh, let us who are but babes rejoice that we are so weak and helpless: this is the very way of acquiring God's strength (II Cor. 12:9, 10).

THE COMPARISON (3, 4).—At first sight there is a great descent from the vastness of the works of God in the heavens to *frail man* (*enoush*), *the son of Adam* (*ben-h'-adam*), whose very name implies that he is of the dust (*Adam*, earthy). How should so great a God visit him? We often confound size and greatness, and forget that the King loves his little babe more than all the splendour and extent of his ancestral palace. The age of the telescope was the age of the microscope. There are as many worlds of wonder which are too minute for our vision as there are which are too great for our understanding.

THE COMPENSATION (5-8).—Yet, notwithstanding his apparent insignificance, man in his original creation was only a little lower than the angels; and he was invested with the vicegerency of the lower orders of creation (Gen. 1:26). Some traces of this power still exist in the power of the human eye and voice over the animals. But sin rolled this crown into the dust. We have to win authority with effort, and retain it with difficulty. We see not yet all thing put under us. But this lost power has been re-acquired by Jesus, as man (Matt. 28:18). And in his kingdom it shall be restored to man (Isa. 11:6-9). And from the redeemed creation shall arise the words with which this Psalm begins and ends (Rom. 8:19-22).

Psalm 9 "WITH MY WHOLE HEART!"

Muth-labben probably refers to the tune to which these words were set. The Chaldee version adds "concerning the death of the champion who went out between the camps," referring the Psalm to the death of Goliath of Gath, whose fate aroused the Psalmist's muse in the review of after-years to a very triumphant pitch. This is the first of the ACROSTIC OR ALPHABETICAL psalms, of which there are nine (9; 10; 25; 34; 37; 111; 112; 119; 145.) Psalm 119 is the most remarkable specimen of this acrostic style of composition. Prov. 31, and Lam. 1; 2; 3; 4 present the same acrostic charatcer. In the Septuagint this Psalm refers to the death of the Divine Son, and recites his victory over death and the grave, and all our foes.

THERE IS A PREDOMINANT NOTE OF PRAISE (1-5, 11, 12, 14).—Let us not praise with a divided, but with a *whole* heart. And we must incite praise by recounting *all* God's works. Let memory heap fuel on the altar of praise. The Lord has indeed rebuked our arch-enemy (*compare* 6 and Zech. 3:1, 2), and his strongholds are now wastes, *come to a perpetual end* (II Cor. 10:4; Col. 2:15). What a contrast between our dead foes, and our ever-living King! (7).

THERE IS AN ASSERTION OF TRUST (7-12, 18).—"Refuge" is *high tower* (R.V.). The oppressed, the humble, the needy, and the poor have strong encouragement. Calamity drives them to God, and makes them familiar with the secrets of his character. The more we know of God the more we can trust Him. Doubt is born of ignorance. Leave God to vindicate you: He will not forget (12).

THERE IS A PETITION FOR FURTHER HELP (13, 19, 20).—What a contrast between the gates of death (13) and the gates of the holy city! (14). What a striking example of 15th verse is given in the story of Haman! (Esther 7:10). He who lifts the righteous hurls down the wicked. It is a sin to *forget* God (17; Isa. 51:13). There is a striking emphasis in the two closing verses; the Hebrew for *men* might be rendered *weak,* mortal man (*enoush*).

Psalm 10 "THOU HAST SEEN! THOU HAST HEARD!"

This Psalm is full of sorrowful complaint, and befits God's people in all seasons of distress.

THE MALICE OF THE FOE IS POWERFULLY DESCRIBED (1-11).—The treatment which the unjust oppressor deals out to his prey is set forth in many rich and striking images. Now it is the serpent with venom under his tongue (7); now, the bandit secreted in ambush (8); now, the lion in his den, and again the hunter snaring the unsuspecting prey (9). And all the while God seems to stand afar off and hide his eyes from the tribulation caused to his own; so much so that all the thoughts of the wicked, that there is no God, seem abundantly confirmed (4, 11).

THE PRAYER OF THE OPPRESSED (12-15).—God is asked to lift up his hand from rest in the folds of his robe. He is the helper of the helpless and hapless, who commit themselves to Him. Let us commit ourselves to Him that judgeth righteously (I Pet. 2:23). It is supposed that the suppliant entreats that the oppressor's boast (11) may be answered in another way than he thinks, in the complete extirpation of every vestige of his sin.

THE BOAST OF FAITH (16-18).—What in Ps. 9:19 was a prayer is here taken as an accomplished fact. Forget not the humble (12) is here recalled: *Thou hast heard the desire of the humble* (17). The preparation of the heart in prayer is His work; and so of course He is able to hear and answer. When we abide in Jesus, and the Holy Ghost flows through our hearts as sap through the vine, we are taught how to pray; and whatsoever we ask we receive. True prayer begins with God, and returns to Him again.

Psalm 11 "THE RIGHTEOUS LORD"

When John Welsh and his fellow-captives were summoned from their prison on the Firth of Forth, to appear before the court, they sang this Psalm as they walked by night under guard to their trial. It is worth reading in the rugged Scotch version. The Psalm is a debate between fear and faith, and probably dates from the time when David was being persecuted by Saul.

THE COUNSELS OF EXPEDIENCY.—(1) Timid friends, anxious for his safety, urged him, not simply to flee to the literal mountains, which he did, but to desert the cause of God, and to renounce his faith—which he never did. Birds escape the dangers of the plains by winging their flight to the caves or woods of the hills. Such counsels of expediency were frequently given to Nehemiah (Neh. 6). And the enemy has ever sought to dislodge the faithful servants of God by fear (Job 2:9, 10; Luke 13:31). Luther's diaries abound in similar references. And there is much force in the reasons alleged. The bow is already being bent; the darkness is in favor of evil stratagems (2, R.V.); and the foundations of social order are undermined. Righteousness cannot avail: why should it not be relinquished?

THE ANSWERS OF FAITH (4-7).—The revolutions of earth cannot shake His throne. He permits the Evil One some license that the righteous may be tested (Job 1, 2; Luke 22, 31, 32). And when the limit is reached which His love apportions to His people's trials, then their persecutors will first be entangled in snares, from which they shall not escape, and then overwhelmed as Sodom was. But in the meantime, whilst in the midst of persecution and sorrow, let the righteous remember that the eye of God not only beholds their patience, but exchanges glances of tenderness with his suffering ones (Exod. 3:7).

Psalm 12 " HELP, LORD!"

The opening words suggest that this Psalm is an appeal for help in bad and evil days. There are days when sin seems rampant, sweeping all before it. The great and godly men one by one are taken away, and the ungodly reign supreme. But when there is no help in man, let us turn to God with the cry which broke from Peter's lips when sinking in the waves. It is a very convenient cry, both from its brevity and its comprehensiveness. *Help, Lord!* (see Micah 7:2).

THE NEED OF HELP (1, 2, 4).—Deceit is specially the sin of Orientals. A double heart is literally *a heart and a heart;* and such practise deceit on neighbors whom they should love. On the contrary, we are bidden to put away lying, and speak truth to our neighbors (Eph. 4:25; Col. 3:9). Oh for perfect transparency of heart and life!

THE CERTAINTY OF HELP (3, 4).—The very prayer begotten in the heart carries the assurance of an answer. Besides, the world is so made that daring wickedness rarely goes unpunished. Let us never act as if we thought our lips were our own; for they too have been bought with the price of those dear parched lips which cried, *I thirst.*

THE ARISING OF HELP (5).—God hears sighs. One sigh will make Him arise, as the sighs of Stephen made Jesus stand (Acts 7:56).

THE BLESSED PROMISE OF HELP (6, 7).—There is no mixture of error in the words of God; all dross has been removed: they may therefore be trusted to the uttermost. Bind the words of God to your heart, and go fearlessly forth into the midst of vile and wicked men: you shall be *kept and preserved* for evermore (Isa. 54:17).

Psalm 13 "HOW LONG, O LORD?"

This Psalm evidently dates from the time of the Sauline persecutions. Four times the afflicted Psalmist cries, *How long?* The Psalm begins in the deepest dejection, but it clears as it proceeds; and the soul, lark-like, rises above the lower current of east wind, till it revels in the heaven of God's love. Pray on, troubled believer: it is marvelous how certainly prayer proves to be a ladder from the deepest dungeon into the most radiant day.

DEPRESSION (1, 2).—Saul's persecutions probably lasted for eight or nine years; and no hope of termination appeared (I Sam. 27:1). David was as a man who spends five hundred days passing through a forest: the tangled over-growth hides the sun; and he begins to despair of ever emerging. Some say that this Psalm is the cry of the Church (Rev. 6:10).

SUPPLICATION (3, 4).—How wise to hand over all worries and anxieties to God. If, instead of carrying them in our own heart, we made them all instantly known to Him, we should live more blessed and peaceful lives (Phil. 4:6, 7). He had bemoaned four evils: he now entreats three blessings (3). Oh for the enlightened eyes! (Eph. 1:18). The holy soul is as eager for God's honor, as for its own vindication (4).

ASSURANCE (5, 6).—It is very delightful when we can sing, though not out of the wood, because so certain of the coming deliverance. Faith praises for the victory, before the fight has even reached its worst. After lying for some time in the Bishop of London's coalhouse, Mr. John Philpot was rebuked for singing hymns in prison, and he answered: "I have so much joy that I cannot lament; but day and night I never was so merry before."

Psalm 14 "THE FOOL HATH SAID—'NO GOD!'"

The creed, character, and doom of the Atheist are here depicted; and the Psalm is so important as to be repeated (53), with slight alterations, which show this rendering more suitable for public use. The Hebrew word translated *fool* (*naval*) denotes one of withered intellect.

THE ROOT OF ATHEISM.—It begins not in the head, but in the heart (Rom. 1:21). Men do not like God; they try to ignore Him, and end by blatantly denying Him. The surest way of dealing with such is to treat them as rebels and sinners.

THE EFFECT OF ATHEISM ON THE CHARACTER (1-6).—Corruption as of a grave; abominable works; darkened understanding; filthiness of heart and life; persecution and shaming of the godly; but finally "great fear." What a terrible catalogue of crimes! These verses are largely quoted by the Apostle (Rom. 3:10-12) as true of all men; because the seeds of this awful crop are by nature latent in us all, awaiting favorable conditions of germination. God comes as a *seeker* ("the Father *seeketh*": John 4:23), eagerly looking for those who abjure the ways of sin, and call upon Him; and these are picked out by Him as his choice jewels, for his own. The word *because* in ver. 6 would be better rendered *but*. The enemy may come up against the camp of the righteous, but God is in the midst of them; they cannot be moved (Ps. 46:1, 5).

THE BEST ANSWER TO ATHEISM (7).—The Church of God, of whom the Jewish people was a type, is too much in captivity to the world and the devil. Let us daily ask that our salvation may speedily come, the advent of which shall bring discomfiture to our foes, and long, glad rejoicings to us (Heb. 9:28; II Thess. 1:6-10).

Psalm 15 WALKING WITH GOD

This Psalm was probably composed with Ps. 24—which it closely resembles—to celebrate the bringing of the Ark to Mount Zion. The first words are almost a repetition of the awe-struck question of the stricken men of Bethshemesh (I Sam. 6:20). And the rest of the Psalm gives a description of those who may dwell with God. If we would have fellowship with God, and dwell in his house all the days of our earthly life, let us see that this character is ours, by the grace of the Holy Spirit!

THE CHALLENGE OF THE SOLOIST (1).

THE ANSWER OF THE CHOIR (2-5).—The answer is given, first, positively (2), and then, negatively (3); so also, in the two following verses. It is very needful that we watch our walk, and work, and talk, if we would have fellowship with God. Those who would walk with God must be like God. We must abhor slander, evil, and reproach. When stories reach us, let them stop with us. Let us act as nonconductors. We must also mind what company we keep; withdrawing from the companionship of the *vile,* but drawing close to and honoring all who *fear* God, as children of the same Father, and therefore brethren and sisters in the same family, whatever their rank or sect. *Usury,* which is a very different thing to the taking of interest; and *bribes*—are equally inconsistent with the vision of God. If only we are heedful of all these matters, we shall not only be able to dwell in the royal palace, as priest and kings, but we shall remain steadfast and unmoveable amid the changes and convulsions around. Here is the secret of permanence and rest (5).

Psalm 16 "MY HEART IS GLAD"

Michtam is derived by some from a word meaning *golden.* And, indeed, that epithet may be truly applied, not only to this Psalm, but to 56, 57, 58, 59, 60. Others explain it as a secret; *i.e.,* a song which leads the holy soul into those deep things of God which are hidden from the wise and prudent, and revealed to babes, by that Spirit who searches them, and loves to make them known to those for whom they are prepared (I Cor. 2:10-14). This, then, is the song of the golden secret.

The key to the Psalm is given by the Apostle Peter, when, quoting from it, he says: "David speaketh concerning Him" (Acts 2:25). And in the following verses he goes on to show that the Psalm could not be true in all its wealth of meaning of David, but of David's Lord (verse 31). And the Apostle Paul makes a very remarkable reference to this Psalm, expressly ascribing it to God's authorship through the Psalmist, and affirming that it spoke of Him through whom all who believe are justified (Acts 13:35-38). But, of course, in a lower sense, each one of us who are one with Jesus may appropriate these golden words.

1. The believer turns from all creature confidence to his God, as his only hope and all-sufficient help. Trust in Him cannot be misplaced. It is an argument which God cannot withstand.

2. The rendering of R.V. is very beautiful "I have no good beyond Thee." Satisfied with God; wanting nothing in wealth or comfort outside Him.

3. The soul that loves God loves the people of God.

4-6. *Contrasted* lots.—The R.V. brings out the sense. Those who exchange the Lord for another god shall have "sorrows multiplied"; those who live in God's favor shall have "a goodly heritage." Fleeing idolatry in every form, the Lord is our portion; He will maintain our lot, assert our cause. The measuring lines are outstretched so as to divide off for us a liberal patrimony; they fall in pleasant places, and our allotment is one facing the sun, and including abundance of water. Oh to be as Levi, whose only portion was God Himself! (Num. 18:20; Lam. 3:24).

7. *Reins* mean inmost thoughts (Ps. 7:9). God often speaks in the quiet heart through the language of thoughts.

8. The one object of life is to do his will and please Him; and He is ever at the right hand to help—nearer than our accusers (*compare* Ps. 109:6, 31).

9. *My glory* interpreted by Peter of "the tongue" (Acts 2:26). Speech is man's glory: therewith he blesses God and teaches his brother.

10, 11. Thus the Lord Jesus might have softly sung to Himself as He descended into the lowest depths of his humiliation. *Hell* here is *sheol;* not the place of torment, but of disembodied spirits. *Thine Holy One, i.e.,* one whom Thou favorest. The path of life is the upward path *to* life. God is at our right hand, and our lot is pleasant here; and ere long we shall be at his right hand, amid everlasting pleasures.

Psalm 17 "I SHALL BE SATISFIED!"

This prayer dates from the Sauline persecutions. In the earlier verses David protests his innocence, and then proceeds to plead for deliverance from his foes, ending with glad anticipations of his vision of God's face. It may have been composed for use at eventide; two at least of its verses point in that direction (3 and 15).

PROTESTATIONS OF INTEGRITY (1-5).—What a comfort to appeal from the accusations of men to the judgment-bar of God! Even if there have been unwise things in the behavior, yet God judges the motive and heart. The Hebrew word "tried" is "melted" (*tzaraph*); as gold is tried in the furnace and found to have no dross. But we can have no hope of preserving our integrity and keeping from the paths of the transgressor unless we avail ourselves of the Word of God to test and direct our goings. Use the Royal Guide-book if you would keep on the King's highway. It is beautiful to notice how David follows up his assertion of having kept in God's ways with the cry that he may still be kept there.

PRAYER FOR DELIVERANCE (6-14).—How safe we are! *As the apple of the eye*: the pupil of the eye is defended by eyelash, lid, brow, bony socket, the swiftly-uplifted hand (*comp.* Zech. 2:8). *Thy wings*: the eaglet is gathered under the wing of the parent bird (Deut. 32:11; Exod. 19:4). The R.V. gives a better sense of 13, 14: "*by* thy sword," "*by* thy hand." What a striking contrast there is between ver. 14 and Ps. 16:5, 11.

GLAD ANTICIPATION (15).—*They* are filled with this world—*I* with Thee: they look for the things of this life—I with the eternal and unseen: they satisfied with children—I with thy likeness (I Cor. 15:49; Phil. 3:21). We shall never be perfectly satisfied with anything less than the beatific vision. Most of that rapturous vision is veiled from sight; but when it shall be unveiled, it will be approved.

Psalm 18 MY ROCK AND MY FORTRESS

There is another form of this Psalm on record—that in II Sam. 22. It recapitulates the deliverances of the past, and sets them to music. The 2nd and 49th verses are quoted in New Testament as the words of the Lord Jesus (Heb. 2:13; Rom. 15:9).

A GOOD RESOLVE (1-3).—How beautiful is this array of metaphors; as if no single one were forcible enough to set forth the many-sided glory of God. And Faith puts its hand, *my*, on all that God is, and claims it for its own. Can *we* not also say: "I LOVE Thee"? Not indeed as we would, yet we can take John 21:17: "Thou knowest." David's word is a very intense one.

THE STORY OF THE PAST (4-19).—It is good to recall God's gracious dealings. David does it in highly poetical language, borrowed from the scenes of the Red Sea and Sinai. And yet there was so much of God's gracious help in his life, that he was warranted in comparing it with the deliverance from Egypt. We, too, have our Red Seas. And God will do for us as much as for David. In our distress let *us* also cry. "Far up within the bejewelled walls, and through the gates of pearl, the cry of the sufferer will be heard." *My cry came before Him.* The voice is thin and solitary, but the answer shakes creation.

THE CLAIM OF THE RIGHTEOUS (20-27).—The righteousness of which David boasted was not his own; for he was willing to admit that he was not free from impurity: but it rather indicates purity of motive and integrity of heart as contrasted with hypocrisy and wickedness. *Compare* 26 with Lev. 26:21-24. Our moral character gives its shape to our thoughts of God.

JOYFUL ANTICIPATION (28-45).—God's way is perfect, and He maketh our way perfect. Walls and troops cannot oppose us, when God's way lies through them, and we are on the line of his purpose. Swift and sure-footed in slippery places (33). Strong in battle (34). Oh, the *gentleness* of God! (35). It has done more for us than severity. Instead of the word "gentleness" the Prayer-book version translates, "Thy loving correction."

THE CLOSING HALLELUJAH (46-50).—We must stint our words when we thank our fellows, lest we be extravagant. But mortal lips need never refrain themselves for fear of saying too much to God.

Psalm 19 THE WITNESS OF THE HEAVENS

The Psalm of the Two Books: the Book of nature, and the written Word. If Psalm 8 were written at night, this must have been penned by day. In the 1st verse God is called EL, the Strong One; in verses 7, 8, 9, 14, the Hebrew name JEHOVAH is translated LORD; as if his glory as Creator were the stepping-stone to loftier conceptions of Him in redemption. From both sources comes the sense of sin.

NATURE.—There is the blue tapestry of the azure, and the expanse of the firmament, woven by God. What a picture of the sacred silence of the dawn! "No speech, nor language; their voice cannot be heard" (R.V.). There is also the universality of their witness-bearing. "Line" is the compass or territory through which they speak; some translate it "chord"; but there is no tongue in which the works of God do not speak. Does not the picture of the dawn, in which the sun comes forth radiant as a bridegroom, strong as an athlete, make us think of the resurrection? And is not Jesus our Sun, from the heat of which no loving heart need be hid? (Mal. 4:2).

REVELATION.—Six synonyms—the law; the testimony; the statutes; the commandment; the fear; the judgments—are used of the Word of God; and twelve qualities are ascribed to it. How truly might our blessed Lord have appropriated verse 10! The man who, as David, lives a simple natural life, is he who best appreciates the Bible.

CONFESSION AND PRAYER (12-14).—"Errors"; the same word is used Lev. 4:2, 13. "Errors" will, if not checked, lead on to presumptuous and deliberate sins. The "dominion" which the Psalmist feared is expressly referred to in Rom. 6;14. What a claim we have on God when we can say, "Thy servant!" For the seventh time David repeats the covenant name "Jehovah," with two last, loving epithets, "Rock" and "Redeemer" (R.V.).

Psalm 20 "THE LORD ANSWER THEE!"

This Psalm may have been written on such an occasion as that of II Sam. 10. It may be used especially when the armies of our King are going forth to war.

THE PRAYER OF THE SOLDIERS (1-4).—Ready drawn up for the fight, the soldiers pray for their king, who was wont on the eve of battle to bring sacrifices and offerings for success. (1) *The Lord hear thee!* literally, *The Lord shall answer thee!* The "name" of God is his character: and the God of Jacob will not reject or forsake any worms as weak as the patriarch was once.

THE RESOLVE (5).—As the banners wave in the breeze it is expressly said that God is the object of trust. The Lord is our banner (Exod. 17:15); and we succeed so far as we set forward in his name and for his glory.

THE VOICE OF THE KING (6).—The devotion of the soldiers seems to their leader an omen for good. God's holiness is a guarantee of his faithfulness. The Hebrew for *strength* (*gevooroth,* "powers) is plural, implying the infinitude of God's resources.

THE FINAL CHORUS OF THE HOST (7-9).—As they look across the field to the embattled array, they contrast the chariots and cavalry of the foe with their slender equipment. But, lo! as they gaze, their enemies are scattered; and with the brief ejaculation, "Save!" they hurl themselves headlong in pursuit.

Psalm 21 STRENGTH AND SALVATION

This is evidently a companion Psalm to the former. The blessings there asked are here gladly acknowledged to have been granted: and bright anticipations are entertained for the future. How much of it is only true of our King! Let us read it over with an especial reference to Him, as He rides forth on his white horse (Rev. 19:11-16).

2. *His heart's desire.*—The *heart's desire* finds its expression by the *lips*: and so the answer comes. There is no contrast implied between unspoken desire and oral prayer: both ascend together.

3. *Thou preventest him* (*goest before him*).— God's help anticipates our needs. It precedes us.

4. *He asked life of Thee.*—Our true life can be measured only by eternal ages.

5. *Honour and majesty*—Similar terms are used of our Lord in Heb. 2:9—"crowned with glory and honour."

6. *Most blessed for ever.*—Blessedly true of our beloved dead (Rev. 20:6).

7. *Trusteth—shall not be moved.*—Trust is the secret of permanence.

8-12. *All thine enemies.*—Our foes, and the foes of Jesus, must perish. Not one of them shall escape. In the garden of Olivet, Christ's gentle *I am He* overthrew the soldiers (John 18:6). How will it be when the wrath of the Lamb flames forth?—who shall be able to stand? (Rev. 6:16). Fear them not! "they are not able to perform." The dog may snarl, but is muzzled.

13. *Be Thou exalted, O Lord!*—Every loyal heart must join in that devout wish. But we may ask whether we have exalted Him to the place of power in the inner kingdom. God has exalted Him to be Prince and Saviour; and we shall not have peace until we have done the same (Acts 5:31).

Psalm 22 THE PSALM OF THE CROSS

The Hebrew inscription to this exquisite ode, which demands as many pages as we can give it lines, is "the hind of the morning." The "hind" stands for one persecuted to death, and is also an emblem of loveliness (Sol. Song 2:7, 9). The cruel persecutors are designated as "bulls, lions, and dogs." Perhaps the addition "of the morning" (*marg.*) refers to the dawn of brighter and better days.

There is a remarkable exchange in the latter part of the Psalm (22-31) of triumph for complaint. Of course, our blessed Lord is in every syllable. Indeed, it reads more as a history than a prophecy. It seems as if the Divine Sufferer recited it to Himself during the agonies of his crucifixion, for it begins with "My God, my God, why hast Thou forsaken me?" and it ends, according to some, in the original, with "It is finished!" "It is the photograph of our Lord's saddest hours: the record of his dying words; the lachrymatory of his last tears; the memorial of his expiring joys." If we have here the sufferings of Christ, we shall certainly have also the glory that should follow.

1-8. Complaints that he is Forsaken and Unheard, although He had Trusted for deliverance.

9-21. Expostulations on the Ground of Past Favor and of the Extremity of His Sufferings.

22-31. Ejaculations of Praise, as the Cloud Begins to Roll Away.

Ah, Psalm that was balm to the pierced heart of Jesus, how precious art thou to those who drink his cup!

1. *My God, my God!*—Uttered by our Lord after the darkness had lasted for three long hours. *His* God still, though hidden. God was as near and tender as ever; but the human consciousness of the Sin-bearer, made a curse for us, had lost the sensible enjoyment of his presence.

2. *Thou hearest not.*—This is rendered in R.V. *answerest not.* God's silence is no reason for our silence; but on the contrary, an incentive to more importunity (Matt. 15:22, 23).

3. *Thou art Holy.*—Though prayer is not immediately answered, there is no imputation on the character of God. The praises of the saints are the throne of the Eternal.

4, 5. *They trusted.*—The thrice repetition is very significant. Is this the prominent feature in our character that our children will recall, and on which they will base their pleas?

7-10. *They laugh me to scorn.*—His very enemies had remarked how *he rolled himself upon God* (8, *marg.*). and used it as a jeer; but the Sufferer turns it into a prayer. From his birth he had been God's nursling, and could he be now deserted?

11. *Be not far from me.*—Trouble sometimes seems nearer than God. But this is only to the eye of sense. Faith descries the Deliverer coming across the waves, and saying, It is I.

14. *All my bones are out of joint.*—What a vivid picture of the anguish of the cross! The gaping crowds; the strength and virulence of their abuse; the bones wrenched from one another; the broken heart; the fevered lips; the pierced hands and feet; the parted garments; the thrusting of Jehovah's sword against his fellow (20; Zech. 13.7).

20. *My Darling.*—We learn from the parallelism that this represents his soul. The Hebrew is *my only one.*

21. *Thou hast heard me.*—In the limits of one verse prayer begins to change to praise. He who had said, "Thou hearest not" (2), confesses that all the while God had been hearing and help-

ing him. The dog, the lion, the wild oxen (R.V.), are emblems of the hatred of man, from which God had rescued his servant.

22. *I will declare thy name.*—John 17:26; Heb. 2:12.

24. *He hath not despised.*—Man may despise (6), but God cannot. Man may abhor a worm (6), but God uses such to thresh mountains. And though his face may seem hidden (1, 2) it is not really so.

25, 26. *My praise shall be of Thee.*—Of Thee, *i.e.*, originating from Thee, shall be my praise. Praise shall be the ultimate perquisite of all who seek God. And all who feed on the words of Jesus must have everlasting life (John 6:51).

27-31. *All the ends of the world.*—There is surely here a forecast of the effects of the death of the cross, first on the Jews (23), but also in these verses on the Gentiles. The ends of the earth converted; the usurper dethroned (28); the resurrection accomplished (29); and the seeing of a spiritual seed to satisfy the travail of the Redeemer's soul.

Psalm 23 THE SHEPHERD PSALM

A Sabbath restfulness breathes through this Psalm. It is the favorite of the children; but the oldest and holiest must confess that it touches an experience which lies still in front of them. There is no strife, no fear, no denunciation of the wicked, no effort at self-vindication: the waters, which fretted and chafed in their earlier course, flow in placid repose through the rich pasture lands, and beneath the arms of the spreading trees; and if for a moment there is the suggestion of the dark valley of deathshadow, it is instantly dismissed by the thought that He will be there, whose face makes light in the darkest night.

Jehovah is represented successively as the true Shepherd and Guide and Host of his people. And we are taught to think much less of ourselves in our relations with Him, and more of Him as being responsible for us. After all, it is not so much a question of what we are to Jesus, as of what He is to us. The flock does not keep the Shepherd, but the Shepherd the flock. Look away from self, and trust Him to keep and lead and feed. All that we should care for, is not knowingly to resist any of his gracious promptings and teachings.

The Psalm was probably written when the sun of David's life was westering. The experience of age is grafted on the memories of youth.

1. *The Lord is my Shepherd.*—The thought of God as the Shepherd of his saints is familiar to Scripture students from Gen. 48:15 to Rev. 7:17, especially John 10. Let God see to your wants. There is nothing you really need for which you may not count on Him.

2. *He leadeth me.*—"Pastures of tender grass and waters of rest."

3. *He restoreth my soul.*—When the soul has spent itself unduly, He recruits it. When diseased, He heals it. When penitent, He puts it back whence it fell. It is only as we look back on life that we see how absolutely right were paths that seemed most wrong. But his name and character are implicated in doing the best for us.

4. *The valley of the shadow.*—This is not death only, but any dark ravine through which we have to pass. But God seems nearest then. It is no longer *He, but Thou.* Club to defend; crook to chasten and guide.

5. *Thou preparest.*—Every day is that table spread with food for body and spirit, but we need the purged eye to see, and the believing hand to appropriate. And we must be prepared to break through a ring of enemies to feed, and to get the daily anointing of the Holy Spirit (I John 2:27).

6. *The house of the Lord.*—God's house is his Presence—Himself. There let us live. And his twin-angels shall follow us. We must not look behind, dreading the pursuit of the evil past. The rear is well protected. Watch-dogs behind; the Shepherd before.

Psalm 24 THE KING OF GLORY

Psalm 22 tells of the Cross; 23 of the Crook; 24 of the Crown. This great choral hymn was evidently composed to celebrate the removal of the Ark from the house of Obed-edom to Mount Zion (II Sam. 6). There must have been a great procession by which it was conducted, with music and song, to its resting-place (I Chron. 15:2-27).

This Psalm was without doubt composed for a choir. The first two verses might have been sung by the entire festal crowd; the third by a single voice; the fourth and fifth by the choir; and the sixth by all. What a sublime challenge on the part of the approaching host is contained in verse 7, answered by a company already within the gates (8); to which again the vast shout of the multitudes gives reply. Surely this ode was rightly employed when used by Handel to represent the return of the ascending Saviour to his home. It never reached its perfect accomplishment till the Victor over hell and the grave arose on high.

1, 2. *The earth is the Lord's.*—These words were chosen by Albert the Good to be placed as a motto over the Royal Exchange. The earth and men are God's by right of creation and redemption. The devil is a usurper, and shall be thrust out.

3, 4. *The Hill of the Lord.*—The Almighty is also the All-Holy. We are his: but we cannot approach Him unless we observe certain conditions, which He will secure in us by the power of the Holy Spirit, if we are only willing that He should.

5. *From Jehovah—from Elohim.*—Ah, what a blessing is this! (Gen. 15:6; 49:25).

6. *Them that seek thy face.*—We must evidently insert the name of God before Jacob, as the margin suggests.

7. *Lift up your heads!*—The doors are *everlasting*, grey with hoar antiquity, and destined to stand for ever.

The connection between Psalms 15 and 24 has already been pointed out.

This Psalm is accomplished in us when Jesus enters our hearts as our King to reign; and it will have its full realization when the earth and its populations welcome Him as its Lord.

Psalm 25 "THE SECRET OF THE LORD"

An acrostic or alphabetical Psalm. The verses begin with the letters of the Hebrew alphabet; probably to aid the memory: so also Psalms 9; 10; 25; 34; 37; 111; 112; 119; 145. It contains many similar expressions, which might be connected by slight Bible markings. Such are *wait* (3, 5, 21); *ashamed* (2, 3, 20); *teach* (4, 5, 8, 9, 12).

1. *Unto Thee, O Lord!*—Lift up your soul, that its darkness may be penetrated by his light, its maladies healed by his saving health.

4, 5. *Lead me! . . . and teach me!*—If you utter this prayer in all sincerity, wait for the answer: be sure that it will come, and if you are not yet told what to do, wait till you know certainly. "Wait all the day."

8, 9. *Therefore will He teach.*—God's holiness is no barrier, but an encouragement to repentant sinners (*compare* Matt. 9:13 and Luke 15:1). Not the meek only, but sinners may claim his teaching. Do not be careful as to your lessons, but as to acquiring them. God will set them; we must get them by heart.

11. *For thy Names's sake!* How much the Old Testament writers count on God's Name! It is his character, his troth, Himself (Josh. 7:9; Isa. 63:14, 16; Ezek. 36:22, 23).

13. *His soul shall dwell.*—In the darkest, saddest hour we may find a home in the goodness of God.

14. *The secret of the Lord.*—What secrets God has to tell his own! (Gen. 18:17; John 13:31; 15:15; I Cor. 2:9, 10).

15. *Mine eyes are toward the Lord.*—Do not look down at your feet, but up to his face.

20. *Oh, keep my soul!*—When we are unable to keep ourselves for God, let us trust Him to keep us for Himself. He is able to do this; and it is best to transfer the entire responsibility to Him (II Tim. 1:12). We cannot be "ashamed" (Isa. 45:17; 49:23; 50:7).

Psalm 26 "JUDGE ME, O LORD"

In some respects this Psalm is similar to the previous one: only, instead of entreaties for forgiveness, there are protestations of innocence. It may have been composed during Absalom's rebellion, and is a strenuous protest against the dissembling and hypocrisy on which that revolt had been built. In these avowals of conscious rectitude, we must ever bear in mind that David did not mean to express absolute sinlessness, but his innocence of those specific charges with which he had been assailed.

1. *I shall not slide.*—If *therefore* be omitted, we get the sense that he had not slidden from his attitude of faith. Let us trust God to keep us trusting.

2. *Examine, and prove.*—These words are all borrowed from the smelting furnace, and point to the purity which fire gives. If the Baptism of Fire avail not, we must pass through the Fires of Purification (Num. 31:23; Mal. 3:1-3).

3. *I have walked in thy truth* (Zech. 10:12).

4, 5. *I have not sat.*—Human society without God is an empty bubble, and cannot satisfy (Psa. 1:1).

6, 7. *In innocency.* —We must use the laver, if we would minister at the altar. It is more important to be clean than to be clever. We must wash before we publish and tell.

8. *I have loved . . . thy house.*—Hatred of evil men (5) is one side of the coin; love to God's house the other. Seek either; and the other will be yours.

11. *Mine integrity.*—Can we also assert our integrity—that is, our whole-heartedness? (Job 2:3, 9; 27:5). Is our eye single? our heart open toward God? Are our motives pure? If so, though we still need "grace to help," yet we are on an even table-land, in which there is no pitfall or cause of stumbling, and from which the glad song of praise shall ascend as sweet incense to God.

Psalm 27 "SEEK YE MY FACE!"

This Psalm probably dates from the time when the exiled king, surrounded by unscrupulous foes, looked from the regions beyond the Jordan to the beloved city, where the Ark of God abode. It would almost seem as if his one thought was—not to resume his throne, but to revisit the sanctuary of God. "One thing have I desired." The "one thing" people are irresistable (Phil. 3:13).

I. ASSURANCE (1-6).—How many-sided is God! He is "light," "salvation," and "strength." The trusting soul lives behind a triple door. We may shrink from uttering the desire to dwell evermore in Jehovah's house. And yet there is a sense in which even busy people can do this, by the grace of the Holy Spirit. God's presence is God's house. Abide in Him! You are "in Him" unless you consciously go out. How beautiful is God's world! How much more beautiful Himself! If you behold that beauty, it will be transferred to your own face, though you wist it not (Psa. 90:17; 110:3). *Temple* (4) is here applied to the tent which David erected on Mount Zion (II Sam. 6:17). The believer who hides in God is as safe as the young Joash (II Chron. 22:12).

II. SUPPLICATION (7-14).—The triumphant trust of the Psalm suddenly changes to a tone of sadness, as if a cloud had for a moment passed over the soul. Did the writer for a moment look from his Saviour to the wind and waves? How true to life are these changing strains! What a comfort to know that our experiences do not alter our standing! Sometimes God seems to hide his face, only to lead the soul to a pitch of trust which otherwise it had never dared to adopt (Mark 7:28). Here is the heart-echo. God's words come back to Him as a prayer. The dearest may forsake, but the Lord *gathers* (Isa. 40:11).

11. *Teach me! . . . lead me!*—Again we have the even path of Psa. 26:12.

12. *Mine enemies.*—We may apply this to the wicked spirits of the heavenly places who assail us, if we have no earthly foes who hate us for the truth's sake. It is an unlikely thing, however, that we should escape hatred, if we are living very near to Christ (John 15:19, 20).

13. *Unless I had believed to see.*—Look up! and look on!

14. *Wait on the Lord!*—It is so much easier to act, or lie down and die, or run to friends, than to wait. But waiting is the true

posture. He that waits for God shall not be long without the God for whom he waits.

How delightful are the *me* and *my* of this exquisite Psalm!—the pronouns of personal appropriation.

Psalm 28 "UNTO THEE WILL I CRY!"

This Psalm also probably belongs to the time of Absalom's rebellion. Verses 2 and 3 closely resemble Psa. 26:8, 9.

1, 2. *If Thou be silent.*—What a thought is suggested in the silence of God! Sometimes He is silent because He loves (Zeph. 3:17, *marg.*). Sometimes to test our faith and stir up our zeal (Matt. 15:23). Sometimes because He has already spoken, and we have not heeded his words (Matt. 26:62). But if a period of silence befall us, let us not have recourse to any unhallowed source of help (I Sam. 28:6, 7): let us rather pray and wait, lifting up our hands for help towards God's oracle.

3-5. *The workers of iniquity.*—The world is so made that wickedness is doomed to failure; and the righteous man is glad when God's righteous government of the world is thus approved. We must look at the punishment of wrong-doing, not only from man's standpoint, but from God's.

6, 7. *He hath heard!*—The answer has already begun to steal into the psalmist's soul. Some herald-ray has announced the coming dawn. Some stray flowers of hope piercing the sod tell of coming spring. The quick ear can tell the pibroch of the Highlanders, though foes engirdle the beleaguered city. "I am helped."

8, 9. *The Lord is my strength.*—Note the contrast between *my* strength (verse 7) and *their* strength (8). Trust is contagious as well as panic. What heart, which has experienced God's help, does not long that all may know the blessed help and salvation of God! *Feed them* (Psa. 81:10, 16). *Bear them* (R.V.; Isa. 63:9; 40:11).

It is thus that prayer clears itself in its utterance, and changes its note to praise; and, as a rising lark, breaks into song as it soars.

Psalm 29 "THE VOICE OF THE LORD"

A perfect specimen of Hebrew poetry, giving a magnificent description of a thunderstorm, marching from north to south of Palestine.

PRELUDE (1, 2).—Addressed to the firstborn sons of light (*marg.*), who stand above the tumult of earth and sky. Heaven is viewed as a temple, the priests of which are angels, clad in holy vestments (II Chron. 20:21; Psa. 110:3).

THE DESCRIPTION OF THE STORM (3-9).—We hear first the low, distant muttering of the thunder. The "many waters" may refer to the Mediterranean, from which the storm arose (3). Coming nearer, the tempest breaks on Lebanon and Sirion, the Sidonian name for Hermon; the cedars of which sway to and fro before the wild fury of the storm. And each thunder peal is accompanied by the zig-zag forked lightning (4-7). The storm passes southwards to the desert Kadesh, and to the rock-hewn cities of Petra. The very beasts are stricken with terror, and the forests are stripped of their leafy dress, so that their ground and floor is discovered.

And in the Temple the gathered worshippers respond to the challenge of nature, and say, "Glory!" "Every whit of it uttereth glory" (*marg.*). Oh that every whit of the inner temple of our hearts, and of the spiritual temple of the Church—each nail, and thread, and splint—might utter that same cry, "Glory to God in the Highest!" The *voice of the Lord* is mentioned SEVEN times, reminding us of the seven thunders of Rev. 10:3.

THE CONCLUSION (10, 11).—God's supremacy is the subject of these closing words. He sits upon the clouds as on a throne or chariot. He is King of Nature and of Grace. He is in the strength of the storm, and in the halcyon peace that breaks out like a smile, when the storm has passed; and He can give both to his people. It has been truly said that the Psalm begins with *Gloria in excelsis!* and ends with *Pax in terris!* "Glory to God" implies "peace on earth."

Psalm 30 "THOU HAST LIFTED ME UP!"

It becomes the child of God to dedicate to Him the house in which he lives, so that each room of it should be part of His temple, dedicated to His service and used for His glory. David wrote this psalm and song on the occasion referred to in II Sam. 5:11. It records the emotions which befitted the transition from the cave of Adullam to the splendor and comfort of a house of cedar.

1. *I will extol Thee!*—Lift Him up in song, who has lifted thee up in mercy. Exalt Him, from each eminence to which He has exalted thee.

2, 3. *Thou! Thou! Thou!*—It may be that David celebrates here his recovery from some deadly sickness. At such times we must not put the physician or remedy in the place of God (II Chron. 16:12).

4, 5. *Sing! . . and give thanks!*—No one saint, though he were a sweet singer like David, always engaged in making melody, could tell forth all God's praise. In what arrears then must most of us be! *Weeping* is here personified; she is a lodger, who tarries for the brief Eastern night, and then, veiled, glides out of the house before daybreak. And with the first ray of light *joy* comes to stay; and there is a shout in the vestibule.

6-9. *I cried to Thee!*—When our circumstances are prosperous, we begin to rest in them rather than in God; and we forget Him, by whom alone our mountain is made to stand strong. Then He hides his face. The Chaldee says, "His sheckinah." And the soul, panic-stricken, turns from the creature to the Creator.

10. "*Lord, be Thou my helper,*" is a prayer which will well befit our life every day. How swiftly the prayer was heard!

11, 12. In these utterances the past tense is used of Him who turneth the shadow of death into morning. Christ might have used these words of rapture on the Resurrection day. Each penitent may use them. And we shall use them when we have put off the body of our humiliation, and stand before God in his sanctuary (I Cor. 15:54, 55).

Psalm 31 "IN THE SECRET OF THY PRESENCE"

In verses 9-18 we have a picture of unusual grief. Some have thought the Psalm was written during the Sauline persecutions; but it is more likely that it dated from the rebellion of Absalom. It alternates from depths of despondency to heights of sublime trust; and well befits the experiences of any who walk in the darkness and have no light (Isa. 50:10).

1. *In Thee do I trust.*—God's answer to his people's trust is guaranteed by his righteousness (Joel 2:26).

2. *A house of defence.*—Hidden with Christ in God, the believer, apparently defenceless, lives, walks, and has his being, within an impregnable defence. You go into the day, enclosed in God, just as God's life is enclosed in you.

3, 4. *Pull me out of the net!*—When we are wholly given up to God, our cause is his, and the honour of his name is at stake (Josh. 7:9). God's *pulls* are sometimes rather sharp.

5. *Into Thine hand!*—The last words of Stephen, Polycarp, Bernard, Huss, Luther, Melancthon, and of many more, and, above all, of our Lord (Luke 23:46; Acts 7:59). The Psalter was our Saviour's prayer-book. This is a suitable petition for every morning, ere we go forth to the day's war and work. What a claim we have on God! He must keep what we commit, because we are his by redemption, and because his truth cannot fail (II Tim. 1:12).

7. *I will be glad and rejoice!*—Faith will find material for her songs in the darkest days. God can recognize us though our beauty has vanished and our friends hardly know us (Job 2:12).

9. *Mine eye is consumed with grief.*—This and the following verses tell a sad tale. There is a special disease of the eyes brought on by excessive weeping; and we all know how the digestion and the health are affected by mental emotion. Yet, amid all, the believer realizes that each moment of suffering is allotted by the dear hand of God. Not one unkind thing can be said or done, unless by his permission. The Refiner sits beside the crucible, his watch in hand, his other hand on the patient's pulse. "My times are in thy hand."

10. *My strength faileth.*—Sin may be committed in the heat of passion; but it lays up for itself bitter memories, and involves sorrowful consequences, which eat into the soul.

11. *A fear to mine acquaintance.*—The inmates of the same house avoided him, and those who met him in the streets without fled from him.

14-18. *Thou art my God.*—What a change there is in the spirit of our life, when we look from men and things to God! Do not look at God through circumstances; but at circumstances through the environing presence of God, as through a golden haze. The times of our Lord's life were in his Father's hands, as ours are in his (15; John 2:4; 7:6, 8, 30; 8: 20). Who will dread the averted faces of friends or foes, if only God's face shines? But we cannot expect it to shine unless, as his servants, we are where He would have us be, and doing his will (16). "Grievous" thing are *hard* ones (18).

19. *How great is Thy goodness!*—As God hath laid up ore in the earth, so that man must dig for it—so hath God laid up unsearchable riches of goodness in Christ, and all spiritual blessings (Rom. 11:33). But we must first know what they are, and then take them (Prov. 2:1-5).

20. *In the secret of Thy presence.*—What a compensation for slandered saints! Perhaps we never know that hiding until we have tasted the proud hatred and contempt of man. Do you know the royal withdrawing room? God's pavilion is sound-tight; the strife of tongues cannot invade.

21. *His marvellous kindness.*—Was this Mahanaim? (II Sam. 17:27).

22. *In my haste.*—It is a mistake to speak in haste.

23, 24. *Oh, love the Lord!*—Oh for love, that we may cast it at His feet, who is so infinitely lovable! And out of love shall spring hope, strength, and courage.

Psalm 32 "THOU FORGAVEST!"

David evidently wrote this Psalm (Rom. 4:6-8). It gives more minutely the story of his experience after his great sin (*comp.*

Psa. 51). *Maschil* means to give instruction. This Psalm was one of Luther's favorites.

1, 2. *Blessed is the man!*—We never realize the blessedness of forgiveness so sweetly as when we have known the burden of unforgiven sin. The word is plural, "*Oh, the blessednesses!*" *Transgression* is passing over a boundary. *Sin* is the missing of a mark. *Iniquity* is what is turned out of its proper course and perverted. The first must be *forgiven, i.e.,* borne away (John 1:29). The second must be *covered, i.e.,* hidden from sight (Rev. 3:18). The third must not be *imputed* (II Cor. 5:19). All these things are true of each believer in Jesus. And in such, forgiveness begets guilelessness.

3-5. *I acknowledged my sin.*—For some time after his sin, the tempter so gagged David that he strove to hide it. Ah, how bitter was his anguish then! He was silent in confession, but not in grief. Under the remorse of conscience he suffered as if the combined agonies of ague and fever had smitten his physical strength, and laid him low. At last he could stand it no longer; but confessed, and experienced the joy of God's forgiveness (I John 1:9). There is no cure for the soul like the heartfelt confession of sin.

6, 7. *For this shall every one . . . pray.*—Godly people should take courage at the Lord's deliverances to their fellows. Godliness is Godlikeness. Do you resemble your Father? (Eph. 5:1). There are times when He seems especially near—nearer than *the floods of great waters.* Oh to be God-enclosed, God-encompassed! Then deliverances, with linked hands, shall encircle us with songs.

8. *I will instruct thee!*—Three precious promises—for instruction, teaching, and guidance. "Though the vision tarry, wait for it" (Hab. 2:3). If the cloud still broods over the Holy Place, do not strike your tents (Num. 9:15-23). Throw on God the responsibility of making his way plain. It is not that God will indicate our duty by the slight movement of the eye, but that He will watch us so as to stop us taking a wrong turn, or making a false step.

9. *The bit and bridle.*—The R.V. gives a more accurate rendering

of the original. With the *bit and bridle* the animal needs to be governed and restrained: we should be actuated by love.

10, 11. *Be glad in the Lord!*—Compassed just now with songs; and here with mercy. When one asked Haydn why his church music was so cheerful, he said, "I cannot make it otherwise: I write as I feel. When I think upon God, my heart is so full of joy that the notes dance and leap, as it were, from my pen." (Phil. 4:4).

Psalm 33 "REJOICE IN THE LORD!"

This Psalm incites to PRAISE. Let us note the subjects enumerated for this holy exercise. Surely it shall not be long ere, touching one of them, our soul shall kindle.

1. *Praise is comely.*—We cannot rejoice in ourselves, but we may in the Lord. Such an exercise is eminently befitting to those who owe to Him all they are and all they hope for.

2. *With harp; with psaltery.*—Sweet-toned instruments and the voice of song will often stir the lethargic soul.

3. *Sing a new song!*—New hearts may use the old words, but ever with fresh emotion.

4. *The word of the Lord, and his works.*—Think of his words of promise and of teaching; and of his marvellous works in creation. Recall his works. Surely in some of these there is food for song. Muse; and the fire must burn (Psa. 39:3).

5. *The earth is full.*—His *goodness* is always passing before us (Exod. 33:19). The evil of the world is due to the devil's intrusion upon God's work (Matt. 13:28).

6-9. *He spake, and it was done.*—In a few words of marvellous power the great work of creation is here recapitulated (Gen. 1).

10-15. *The counsel of the Lord.*—God's providential government. We may know the riches of the glory of his inheritance in the saints (Eph. 1:18; Titus 2:14), and drink in the blessedness of verse 12. The 15th verse does not mean that all hearts are alike, but that all are equally fashioned by his hand (*see* R.V.).

16-19. *No king saved by a host.*—We may not be possessed of a host, or of much strength, or of horses: we may be humble and despised: and yet we need not regret the absence of all these earthly things. They do not really avail in the day of battle. God's unslumbering eye sees our need; and if we only dare to trust in Him, He will deliver us from *death* and *famine.*

20-22. *Our soul waiteth.*—Let us patiently tarry our Lord's leisure, and occupy ourselves as we do so with glad songs of praise for what He is going to do. Trust is certain to bear fruit in joy. The grave must lead to the songs of the resurrection morning. And we may well begin to rejoice in the prospect of joy, and to praise for the praise which we shall be shortly offering.

Psalm 34 "THIS POOR MAN CRIED"

The event which this Psalm celebrates is recorded in I Sam. 21. The association with Achish was not a very creditable incident. David, however, realizes the goodness of God, in spite of his own failures and mistakes. The Psalm clearly falls into two divisions, the first ending at verse 10. In the original, the verses begin with the letters of the Hebrew alphabet.

1. *At all times . . . continually.*—It is a sign of great grace to bless always, in dark times as well as in bright.

3. Let us exalt His name!—We learn from I Sam. 22:9-11, who they were to whom David spoke. "Birds," says Trapp, "when they come to a full heap of corn, will chirp, and call in their fellows." Charity is no churl.

4-6. *This poor man cried.*—Whilst feigning madness, his soul was going up in prayer: we can never turn our faces to God to be disappointed.

7. *The Angel of the Lord.*—*Compare* Acts 12:6-10.

8. *Oh, taste and see.*—Some experiences must be realized before they can be understood. And even then they cannot be expressed: the rapture is unspeakable. But however rich the provision of God's goodness, it will avail nothing until we open eye and mouth.

10. *They that seek . . . shall not want.*— "We will leave thee nothing," said plundering soldiers to a widow, "to put in thee or on thee." "I care not," said she: "I shall not want as long as God is in the heavens." Columba spent his last afternoon in tran-

scribing this Psalm, saying when he reached this verse, "I will stop here. The following verse will better suit my successor."

11-14. *Hearken unto me!*—The purport of this exhortation is well summed up by Peter in his First Epistle (3:10). We need not fret to defend ourselves, or answer false accusations: let us refrain our lips, and go on doing what is right and good. So shall we find our needs supplied, our enemies silenced, and our soul redeemed.

15. *The righteous.*—Those who stand before God accepted in the Righteous One, and in whose hearts his Spirit is working righteousness.

17. *Delivereth them.*—Not kept from it, but delivered out of it (II Cor. 1:10).

18. *The Lord is nigh.*—You may not realize it, oh broken-hearted sufferer, but the great Gardener passes by those who are standing erect, to stoop over thee, beaten down by the storm and trailing on the ground. He comes where He is most needed.

20. *He keepeth all his bones.*—The literal fulfilment of these words must be sought in John 19:36. But there is a sense in which the integrity of our bodily health is due to the perpetual exercise of God's care.

22. *The Lord redeemeth.*—All through these latter verses it is good to note the present tenses of our God's deliverances.

Psalm 35 "WHO IS LIKE UNTO THEE?"

This psalm dates from the Sauline persecution; or else from the disturbed state of the kingdom in David's later days. Each of the three divisions into which the Psalm naturally falls ends with praise (9, 18, 28).

Continually in this Psalm we meet with imprecations on the wicked. The spirit of the New Testament teaches us a higher law, the law of love and forgiveness (Luke 9:55, 56). But perhaps it is better to read these verses as predictions: thus, "Let them be confounded," would read, "They will be confounded." Much of it could be only true in its deepest sense, when uttered by the Messiah: rejected by Pharisee and Scribe; unconscious of any personal hatred; and only prompted by an absorbing passion for the vindication of the righteousness of God.

3. *I am thy salvation.*—What a thrill passes through the soul, when God whispers this assurance—"I am thy salvation!" God Himself is even more to us than what He has done. He is in us; around us; for us: and *He* is our salvation.

5. *The Angel of the Lord.*—This is He who apeared to Abraham, and accompanied the wilderness-march. How awful that He should be wrath and pursue!

7. *Their net in a pit.*—"The pit-net was a pit covered over by the hunter with a net and with twigs, to ensure the fall and capture of a wild beast."

9, 10. *My soul shall be joyful.*—We are apt enough to pray, and not always so careful to return thanks. "Who is like unto Thee?" is a snatch from the song at the Red Sea (Ex. 15:11).

11. *They laid to my charge.*—"They ask me of things that I know not" (R.V.). The idea being that his enemies sought to elicit by questions some ground for accusation (Mark 14:55; Luke 11:53; John 18:19).

12-14. *But as for me.*—How true this was of the Lord Jesus; weeping, praying, dying for his foes (Luke 19:41-44). When our prayers and tears cannot avail for others, they return to bless ourselves (Matt. 10:13). "Darling" is *soul* (17).

20. *The Quiet in the Land.*—This was the title adopted by holy men in Germany through long and dark days; and is beautifully significant of the course of those whose life is hidden with Christ in God.

22. *This Thou hast seen.*—What a striking contrast between God's seeing, and the seeing of the previous verse, directed towards the fall and destruction of the persecuted one!

24. *Judge me, O Lord!*—It is a comfort to appeal from the judgments of men to the bar of God; and to claim his interposition and vindication—which must come, though years pass on without an answer.

28. *My tongue shall speak of Thy praise!*—What might not life

be, if this were our resolution! Such is the spirit of heaven: of its inhabitants it is said, "they rest not day and night" (Rev. 4:8).

Psalm 36 "THY LOVING - KINDNESS"

By the inscription we are specially led to think of SERVICE in connection with this Psalm. The Lord's service is indeed blessed, and it constitutes perfect freedom. Christ's household servants all become nobles.

CONTRASTED SERVICE (1-4).—When there is "no fear of God before the eyes," a man is free to "flatter himself in his own eyes." It is a terrible thing when a man becomes headstrong in wickedness, and abhors not evil.

THE MASTER'S CHARACTER (5-8).—All natural symbols fail to set forth the glories of Nature's Lord. We cannot scale his heights, or plumb his depths, or see his last star. His loving-kindness is precious (I Pet. 2:7). If you want men to leave other refuges, so as to shelter under the wings of God, begin to talk of His love: *that* will draw them (8). Those who thirst for creature-delights have yet to learn something of the meaning of this abundant satisfaction (John 10:10). God gives sorrow by cupfuls, and pleasures by riverfuls. The Hebrew word for *Pleasures* is "Eden."

9. *In Thy light shall we see light.*—The deepest teachings of the Apostle John lie folded in this marvellous verse, as the forest in the acorn (John 1:1-16; I John 1:1-7).

THE SERVANT'S PRAYER (10-12).—Set thy loving-kindness abroach, so that we may drink, and drink again; start the flow, that it may be like some fountain of oil, which, the more it is drawn upon, the more it yields. The man who knows God is "upright in heart"; and *vice versa.* But the servants of sin incur irrevocable ruin, while the servants of God stand in their integrity, unmoved (Isa. 54:17).

Psalm 37 "FRET NOT THYSELF!"

Written by David in his old age (25), this Psalm contains his mature experience. Like Psalms 25, 34, 119, and some others, it is, in its arrangement, an *acrostic* of an alphabetical character. It deals with the great problem of the prosperity of the wicked, as contrasted with the afflictions of the righteous; and shows that these afflictions are only temporary, and that, if we can trust and wait, we shall see that God will mete out their deserts to all. This Psalm is a protest against querulous complaint, and has in all ages been peculiarly dear to the troubled believer. It is exquisitely paraphrased by Gerhardt's noble hymn, "Commit thou all thy griefs." Verse 5 was frequently quoted by Dr. Livingstone.

1. *Fret not.*—This key-note is thrice repeated (1, 7, 8). It might be translated "Do not worry."

5. *Roll thy way upon the Lord* (marg.): see also for same Hebrew word Psa. 22:8, "trusted"; Prov. 16:3, "commit."—True religion is summed up in two words, SUBMIT *and* COMMIT.

7. *Rest in the Lord!* (marg., *Be Silent!*)—The Rhone rids itself of silt as it passes through the still waters of Geneva's lake. It is so much easier to act than to be still.

9. *Earth* may be read *the land*: see also 11, 22, 29, 34, and Matt. 5.:5.—This surely means the supply of all temporal needs as well as of spiritual blessing.

12. *The wicked plotteth.*—Let us not fear the threatenings of our foes. "If God be for us, who can be against us?" (Rom. 8:31).

18. *The Lord knoweth.*—It is enough that God knows what lies hid in each day, and guarantees a sufficiency of strength (Deut. 33:25).

19. *Not ashamed in the evil time.*—So God cared for Jeremiah in the time of siege (Jer. 37:21).

23. *The steps . . . are ordered.*—Jehovah guides the steps and orders the goings. There is safety here (*see* 31; Job 34:21; Psa, 17:5; 40:2; Prov. 16:9).

24. *The Lord upholdeth.*—The Douay version reads "The Lord putteth his hand under him."

25. *I have been young, and now am old.*—Though this may have been David's experience, yet it does not follow that it is universally true. But on the whole it it true. Not the blessedness of the seed of a good man(26).

30, 31. *The law of his God in his heart.*—This is the portrait of the godly as to their life, and heart, and steps. Here, as in Psa. 1 and Psa. 119, the "law of the Lord" is the source of strength and safety. "Thy word have I hid in mine heart" (Psa. 119:11).

34. *He shall exalt thee.*—The fulfilment of these promises depends on our fulfilment of the conditions of faith and waiting. *Because they trust in Him* (40).

37. *The end of that man is peace.*—Bishop Coverdale's translation in the Prayer Book version is worthy of note: "Keep innocency, and take heed unto the thing that is right; for that shall bring a man peace at the last." But the Revised Version favors the ordinary reading. The day may break stormily; but the storms expend themselves ere nightfall, and the sunset is golden.

Psalm 38 "FORSAKE ME NOT!"

One of the seven penitential Psalms. It seeks to bring to God's remembrance his apparently forgotten suppliant (*see* Septuagint heading). We all should have times of calling to remembrance, when we summon back the past.

1. THE BURDEN OF THE PSALMIST'S PRAYER.

2-8. HIS FIRST PLEA, *derived from his physical and mental sufferings.*—Sin's convictions are as arrows. When God's holy law is driven home by the Spirit, we are like hunted deer. Many images are introduced: the hunted quarry (2); disease (3); the waters rolling over a drowning man (4); a burden which crushes the bearer to the ground (4); ah, how blessed that they were not too heavy for the Sin-bearer! (Isa. 53:4, 5; I Pet. 2:24). *I am troubled* might be rendered *I writhe* (6). *Mourning* will soon be exchanged for *singing* (Psa. 40:3).

9-12. HIS SECOND PLEA, *derived from his ill-treatment by men.*—God reads the unspoken sorrows of our hearts (9). Mark the beating, palpitating heart; the failure of strength; the lack-lustre eye (10). When enemies are nearest, friends are furthest: so it was with our blessed Lord (Matt. 26:56). Malice in deed, and malice in thought (12).

13-20. HIS THIRD PLEA, *derived from his absolute dependence on God.*—It is well to be deaf to calumny, and dumb in self-vindication (I Sam. 10:27). Let God undertake your cause (15). How truly might the Messiah have appropriated many of these words! (John 15:25; Matt. 26:62).

21-22. His Closing Petitions.—Thus, faith becomes expectant and triumphant, claiming God as its salvation.

Psalm 39 "I WAS DUMB!"

Written by David and handed to Jeduthun, who is specially mentioned as entrusted with the Psalmody (I Chron. 16:41, 42). Psalm 37 is a calm meditation on the respective lots of righteous and wicked men: this Psalm is full of impetuous and impatient complaint, which finally works itself out, and subsides into a more submissive and plaintive tone.

Impatient Murmurings (1-6).

Faith and Prayer (7-13).

1. *I will take heed.*—A tale of the fifth century tells of a plain man, who, having learned this verse, took leave of his teacher, saying he would return for more when he had mastered it, and did not return for forty-nine years, as he found it took him all that time to acquire its lessons. We need to ask God to tame what man never can (James 3:2-8).

3. *While I was musing.*—The pent-up fire broke forth as from a volcano. Perhaps it had been better, if it had been altogether restrained (Job 1:22; 2:10; 3:1). And yet, if the lips must tell the unsupportable agony of the heart, it is better to tell it all out into the ear of God.

5. *My days as an hand-breadth.*—Not only does he, with all his days, shrink into nothingness in contrast with God, but every man, when standing most firmly, is only "a breath" (R.V., *marg.*), curling up for a moment in the chill air, and gone.

6. *In a vain show.*—What a description of the frailty and vanity of human life! "Walketh as a shadow" (R.V., *marg.*) :*i.e.*, the outward life and activity of men is fleeting and unsubstantial, as the shadow of a cloud on the mountain slope.

7. *My hope is in Thee!*—David ceases from peering into

dizzy depths, which well-nigh make him reel—and looks upward. This is the turning point of the Psalm. The former thoughts are repeated; but the dark clouds are shot through with light.

9. *I was dumb.*—Dumbness not now from wrath, as in 2, but from trust. *Thou didst it.*

11. *When Thou . . . dost correct.*—The transience of human life is now seen to be due to the sin which needs correction, much more than to any defect in God's creative love.

12. *A stranger with Thee* (Lev. 25:23).—We have a constant companion. God is our fellow-pilgrim. "Life need not be lonely, if He be with us; nor its shortness sad."

Psalm 40 "LO, I COME!"

Though the primary reference be to the individual believer, yet there is One only in whom these words can find their entire fulfilment. This is put beyond all doubt by Heb. 10:5-9.

THANKSGIVING (1-3); DECLARATION (4, 5);

CONSECRATION (6-10); ENTREATY (11-17), unite to fill this precious Psalm with helpful thoughts and words.

1. *Waiting, I waited* (marg.).

2. *A pit of roaring*, a deep cavity through which roaring waters rush (Isa. 17:12). *Miry clay* (Psa. 69:2).

3. *A new song.*—May not these have been the words of Christ as He ascended out of the grave, leading the new song which only the redeemed can learn? (Rev. 14:3).

5. *Many are Thy wonderful works.*—What wonderful works in Redemption, Adoption, Pardon, Sanctification, and Providence! God's living thoughts of us pass our power of counting (Psa. 139:17). Here is a maze, in which, bewildered, we may soon lose ourselves.

6. *Sacrifice . . . Thou didst not desire.*— The bloody and unbloody offerings respectively. Where these expressed a loving, obedient heart, they were gladly accepted: otherwise they were valueless (Psa. 50:5; I Sam. 15:22; Hos. 6:6).

Mine ears hast Thou digged (marg.) (Exod. 21:6; Deut. 15:17). —Thus did Jesus freely give Himself up to obedience and bloodshedding for us; and so should we give ourselves irrevocably to Him.

7, 8. *Lo, I come!*—It is blessed when God's law is not only in the head but in the heart; and when it is there it will not be concealed (10).

9. *In the great congregation.*—We are reminded of John 17:26.

10. *I have not hid.*—What themes are here, not only for the Lord, but for his ministers!

12. *Innumerable evils.*—If applied to our Lord, these must be the sins of the whole world (Isa. 53:4-6).

15. *Their shame.*—For a reward of the shame with which they tried to load the sufferer.

16. *The Lord be magnified!*—What a contrast in the objects of those who seek! (14,16).

17. *I am poor and needy.*—The thoughts of God towards the soul (5) are sweet themes of encouragement (1 Peter 5:7). Poverty and need are not barriers to, but arguments for, the thoughts of God.

Psalm 41 "MINE OWN FAMILIAR FRIEND!"

It is supposed by some that this Psalm was composed during the four years in which Absalom's conspiracy was being hatched. Perhaps the pain and sorrow of David's heart brought on some serious illness, which his enemies used for their own purposes, and exulted over with unseemly glee. His sensitive nature is keenly hurt, and pours out its complaint. And we cannot but feel the applicability of the Psalm to Him who was betrayed by his friend. Verse 9 is expressly quoted as fulfilled (John 13:18).

1-3. A General Principle.—When the writer's enemies were in sorrow, he was very tender in his dealings with them (Psa. 35:13, 14). And now he claims that God should do to him as he had done to others.

To make the bed is to *turn it.*—As a gentle nurse alters the sufferer's position and pillows, so does God interpose alleviations for our pains.

4. WHAT A WHOLESOME PRAYER!—

"Heal us, Emmanuel! we are here,
Waiting to feel thy touch;
Deep-wounded souls to Thee repair,
And, Saviour, we are such."—*Cowper.*

5-9. DAVID'S TREATMENT BY HIS FOES.—His disease drew no pity, but only impatience that he lingered so long. Their comforting words were full of deceit; they rejoiced in every symptom of his approaching end. "The man of my friendship," the Ahithophel or Judas of my love, like a vicious mule or horse, has kicked at the sick lion.

10-12. The earlier verses savour more of the Old Testament spirit than of the New. But the conception of ver. 12 is very beautiful, as of a courtier who stands ever in the presence-chamber of the king (II Chron.9:7; I Kings 17:1; Luke 1:19).

13. This Doxology closes the first book of the Psalter. Each of the five books ends in a somewhat similar manner.

Psalm 42 "AS THE HART PANTETH!"

This Psalm embalms the holy musings and yearnings of the exiled king during the rebellion of Absalom. The thoughts are evidently David's, even though their expression and setting may be by the sons of Korah (II Chron. 20:19). This Psalm was a great favorite with the early Christians hunted to the catacombs, where the hart is a common emblem on the walls.

1. *As the hart panteth.*—The hind in the drought, and the hunted stag, long for cool streams. This thirst for God proves the very being of God; for all natural appetites must have their perfect satisfaction.

2. *For the living God!*—Not a dead idol, but the living God of my life. *Lit.* "Appear before the face of God" (Psa. 41:12).

3. Where is thy God?—Shimei's words clung to his memory (II Sam. 16:8).

4. *When I remember.*—The thought of the sufferer is to give a loose rein to these bitter memories, and to allow his sad thoughts to work out their will; and so he recalls the festal processions that he had led in happy bygone days.

5. *Why art thou cast down?*—Thus does the spirit rebuke the flesh, and battles with its despondency in the name of the most High. "David chideth David out of the dumps," says Trapp. Omit *for* from the last clause, which gives a beautiful name for God. Sing, though just now your feet may be fast in the stocks (Acts 16:25).

6. *My soul is cast down.*—These words reappear (Jonah 2:7; Matt. 26:38). You may be excluded from God's temple; but you can always remember God. The Hermons belonged to the trans-Jordanic tribes. And how insignificant was Mizar compared with Zion!

8. *His loving-kindness.*—Tears day and night (3); and yet loving-kindness and song day and night (Job 35:10). Does God sing beside his sufferers? (Zeph. 3:17).

Psalm 43 "GOD, MY EXCEEDING JOY!"

This, with the preceding Psalm, forms a pair.

1. *Judge me, O God!*—When others fail to understand our motives, we may appeal to the righteous bar of God. He is our great Advocate, who will plead for us (Lam. 3:58).

2. *Thou, the God of my strength!*—"The God of my life" (Psa. 42:8) is here "the God of my strength." How fertile is the soul in its epithets for God! And how conclusive the answer to the taunt of the foe, "Where is thy God?" God is with me—in me —here.

3. *Let them lead me.*—Light and Truth in the van; Goodness and Mercy bringing up the rear. Watch them as these twin angels emerge from God's home to conduct the suppliant thither.

4. *God my exceeding joy.*—The altar of outward symbolism and rite was very little to David. It was for God that his soul yearned. How he dwells on that precious name, *God! my God!*

5. *Why disquieted?*—It is a mistake to allow aught to break the inner Sabbath. Troubles may burst on the bulwarks of the ship; but they should not enter its inner sanctuary.

In these Psalms, notice how God is described as the strength of our life; the gladness of our joy; the health of our countenance.

And mark how faith chases the tear from the eye; the furrow from the brow; the fear from the soul.

Psalm 44 "THOU ART MY KING, O GOD!"

This Psalm is so like Psa. 60, that it was probably occasioned by the same circumstances. While David was fighting with the Syrians, the Edomites made an incursion. Amid the anguish of the time this Psalm may have been composed by the sons of Korah. David's return was God's answer to their cry (II Sam. 8:13, 14). Some, however, consider the Psalm to have reference to the events narrated in II Chron. 20.

It well befits any period of the Church's history when her former prosperous condition contrasts sadly with her depressed and suffering state. Rom. 8:36 points the application of verse 22.

Thou hast helped us (1-3). Thou must help us (4-8). Thou art not helping us (9-16). We are not conscious of having done aught to forfeit Thy help (17-22). We invoke Thy help (23-26).

3. *Thy right hand* (Deut. 8:7-18).—All that we are, and have, and hope for, is the gift of God's undeserved mercy. We need not boast; but we need not fear to lose.

4. *Thou art my King!*—We cannot expect deliverances till we have made Christ our King.

8-10. *In God we boast all the day.*—Sometimes God takes away all sensible enjoyment and encouragement, to see whether we still cling to Him for Himself. Happy are we if we can adopt verse 18.

20, 21. *If we have forgotten* (Josh. 22:22).

22. *For Thy sake are we killed.*—The path to victory lies through death and the grave.

23. *O Lord, arise!*—Though the Lord seem to sleep, it is in the stern of the boat. Do not be afraid. If He is with you, no storm can prevail to your destruction (Mark 4:40).

Psalm 45 " THINGS TOUCHING THE KING "

The inscription of this exquisite Psalm, *To the chief musician,* indicates that it was intended to be employed in God's service.

Therefore, though it was probably suggested by Solomon's marriage with the daughter of Pharaoh, we must pass beyond the mere outward interpretation to consider these glowing words in their relation to Christ and his Church. The Psalm is distinctly applied to Him (Heb. 1:8); and the union between Him and his people is often described in such imagery (II Cor. 11:2; Eph. 5:23). Let us pray for the time when the universe shall ring with this marriage-ode: when the hour of the marriage of the Lamb shall have come, and heathen nations partake the joy (Rev. 19:7). *Shoshannim* means "lilies," and tells of the purity of heart that is appropriate to this song of love.

1. *My heart overfloweth* (R.V.)—Oh for the heart, like a geyser, kept ever bubbling over with love for Jesus! We should *make things* about our King—be weaving chaplets—be composing hymns. When the heart is full, there will be no difficulty about the tongue (Acts 2:4).

Here is "good matter" indeed. Christ's beauty (2); his victorious might (4); his Divine nature and everlasting reign (6); his joy (7); his sweetness (8); his bride (13); the splendour of the royal procession (15); the number and royalty of his posterity (16).

2. *Fairer than the children of men.*—Happy are they who live in His presence (I Kings 10:8; Luke 4:22).

3, 4. *In Thy majesty.*—These imperatives are predictions of what the King will do. Though His plans are made, prayer is required to put them in operation. *Because of truth* means *in the cause of truth.* Our King fights for us, and conquers Death, Satan, and the Grave. We march to victory over a fallen foe.

7. *The oil of gladness.*—Here is the secret of perennial joy. So far as we enter into Christ's spirit, we shall share in his joy, a joy such as our fellows cannot know.

8. *All Thy garments.*—The word *smell* might be omitted. The royal robes are as sweet as if they were made of myrrh.

10, 11. *Hearken, . . . and consider!*—Those are likeliest to know the preciousness of Christ's love who, in an abandonment of surrender, cut the cords which would bind them to old and worldly connections, and hold them back from Him. Be only for Christ: so shalt thou taste his secret love.

13. *All glorious within.—Within* is in contrast to *out* of the palaces (8), and refers to the interior of the royal residence. Is there not also a reference to the hidden beauties of Christian character?

17. *Thy name!*—Let us pass on that precious "Name," that the people may break forth into praise in all ages and all climes.

Psalm 46 "BE STILL!"

The historical occasion of this Psalm cannot be certainly determined. But it is very probable that it was composed when Jerusalem was beleaguered by Sennacherib's hosts (Isa. 37). It befits every era in which the Church is in danger from her foes, and it foretells the final destruction of Antichrist. It was Luther's favorite, and is rendered into verse in his memorable hymn, *Ein feste Burg.* During the sitting of the Diet of Augsburg he sang it every day to his lute, standing at the window, and looking up to heaven.

The theme, the security of God's people amid storms, is elaborated in three divisions, at the end of each of which *Selah* recurs.

1-3. *God our Refuge.*—These words may have inspired Hezekiah's address to the captains (II Chron. 32:7). We never know how near God can be till we are in trouble. *Mountains* stand for the most stable things on which we have been wont to fix our confidence. The roaring of the restless sea may well strike with panic the heart which has not got into the covert of its refuge —God.

4-7. *There is a river.*—In opposition to the raging of the sea is the even flow of the pellucid river. Alone among great cities Jerusalem lacked a river; but God Himself was all to her that a river was to ordinary cities (Isa. 33:21). The "river" throughout Scripture, from Eden to the New Jerusalem, is a symbol of the presence of God. The *margin* (5) gives a beautiful alternative reading: "When the morning appeareth." Distress, in the case of God's people, is limited to a night's stay. But probably there is an allusion to Isa. 37:36. God is never before his time, and never a moment too late (Matt. 14:25). If Jehovah is willing to be known as Jacob's God, I too may claim Him, though I be but a worm (Isa. 41:14).

8-11. *He maketh wars to cease.*—War in the Church and the world is doomed, and shall become an extinct art before the Gospel of the love of God. We must cultivate the habit of stillness in our lives, if we would detect and know God.

Psalm 47 "KING OVER ALL THE EARTH"

This Psalm probably dates from II Chron. 20. Without a battle, Israel obtained a victory. They stood still and saw the salvation of God, given in answer to King Jehoshaphat's prayer. The Korhites, whose name is inscribed above it, are expressly mentioned as having been present (19). Before the people left the field, they held a thanksgiving service in the valley of blessing (26). From that valley God is depicted as having made his ascent to heaven, having wrought deliverance for his people (5). This Psalm was probably sung in that "valley of blessing." It is a double call to praise, addressed first to the heathen (1-4), and next to Israel. The name *Elohim* occurs seven times.

1-4. *Oh, clap your hands!*—In these days of world-wide evangelization, the Gentile peoples are beginning to respond to this invitation.

3. *He shall subdue!*—If He can subdue nations, surely He can give us the victory over our sins.

4. *He shall choose!*—Let God choose for you. He will do the best for his beloved.

5. *Gone up with a shout!*—An anticipation of the Ascension (Psa. 68:18).

6. *Sing praises to God!*—Let no heart be cold, no tongue be dumb. Holy songs stir the spirit.

7. *God is the King!*—God claims the kingdoms of this world, which is in revolt; but the end is sure (Rev. 11:15).

8. *The throne of His holiness.*—Holiness is the basis of God's rule.

9. *The shields of the earth* are the princes, as protectors of the people (Hos. 4:18, *marg.*). *Compare* Rev. 21:24.

Psalm 48 "ZION THE JOY OF THE WHOLE EARTH"

This Psalm was probably composed on the same occasion as the foregoing: but *that* was sung in the valley of Berachah; and *this* on the return to Jerusalem and the temple (9). Tekoa (II Chron. 20:20) was only three hours' march from the city, and commanded an extensive view, so that verses 4, 5 were literally true. Let the reader turn to II Chron. 20:27, which tells the occasion of this burst of jubilation. There is also a special connection between verse 7 and the circumstances described in I Kings 22:48; II Chron. 20:37.

The divisions are easy: the dignity and beauty of Jerusalem, as the city of God (1-3); the special instance of Divine deliverance is gratefully recorded (4-8); glad thanksgivings (9-11); and exhortations to commemorate God's goodness to coming generations (12-14).

1, 2. *The city of our God.*—Zion was the heart and centre of the holy city, which clustered around its northern slopes. The Church is the city of God now, in which He dwells, and is known for a refuge.

3. *God . . . a refuge.*—The grandest palace without God is no refuge for the weary, hunted soul. But a hovel becomes a palace if God is known and loved there.

5. *They . . . hasted away.*—Notice the magnificent brevity of this verse. As if one glimpse of that city struck them with panic.

7. *Thou breakest the ships.*—The destruction of the foe was as sudden and total as the sinking of a vessel struck by a cyclone.

8. *As we have heard.*—Whatever God has done in former days, He is able and willing, if needs be, to do again.

9. *We have thought.*—Let us cultivate the habit of holy musing on this sweet and boundless theme.

13. *Mark ye well!*—Consider God's wonderful dealings with his people. Their choice, redemption, adoption, sanctification, eternal inheritance—each is a subject for marking well and pondering.

14. *Our God forever.*—Let us replace the *our* by *my;* and bind this text as a jewel on our heart.

Psalm 49 "THEY THAT TRUST IN WEALTH"

The subject of this Psalm is the prosperity of the wicked, as contemplated by the righteous. This was a frequent cause of wonder to these Hebrew thinkers (*compare* Psa. 37). And the singer presents to us the only consolation within the reach of those times—that the glory and success of the ungodly were but temporary, and would pass away as a shadow; whilst the righteous might count upon long vistas of unbroken blessedness in the presence of God.

We may divide thus: The introduction (1-4); the argument (5-15); the conclusion (16-20).

4. *I will open my dark saying.*—The Psalmist has no hesitation in asking for universal audience; because he not only speaks what he has heard with the ear—he brings forth in song what he has learned from God. There is melody in God's darkest sayings.

5. *Wherefore should I fear?*—The second clause might be better rendered, "When the iniquity of my treaders-down compasses me about."

6-9.*They that trust in wealth.*—Men are very foolish to take airs on themselves, because they are rich. After all, money cannot do much for its owners. It will not enable a man to redeem either his brother or himself from untimely or sudden death. "A million of money for a moment of time!" cried Queen Elizabeth on her deathbed. (*See* I Tim. 6:17).

10-12. *Leave their wealth to others.*—And yet, though wealthy and wicked men are surrounded by death, they try as much as possible to ignore it, and endeavor to obtain immortality for themselves in this world by the perpetuation of their names on their estates.

14. *They are laid in the grave.*—The idea here is of a flock of sheep, with death as shepherd, conducting them to the fold of the grave and *sheol.* What a contrast to Psa. 23:1! The morning

of resurrection glory is not far away, with its songs of triumph: lift up your heads, your redemption draweth nigh.

18-20. *While he lived.*—Our Lord's parables are the best commentary on these words (Luke 12:19; 16:25).

Psalm 50 "I AM GOD, THY GOD"

Asaph is named as the author of this Psalm. Perhaps he who is mentioned I Chron. 15:17, 19, and in II Chron. 29:30. The Psalm contains a severe rebuke of the hypocrite who contents himself with giving a mere outward obedience to the ritual of God's house, but withholds the love and homage of his heart.

In the earlier part God is represented as coming again, as once at Sinai, but now to vindicate and explain the spiritual requirements of his holy law (1-6); then the errors in observing the *first* table are discovered (8-15); after which the Psalmist indicates the violations of the *second* table (16-21); finally there is an impressive conclusion (22, 23). The Psalm is very interesting, because showing how the devout Israelites viewed the Levitical ritual as being only the vehicle and expression of the yearnings and worship of the spiritual life, but not of any value apart from a recognition of God's claims on the devotion of his people.

1. *Elohim Jehovah . . . called the earth.*—God still calls the earth through the Gospel of Jesus.

5. *Gather my saints together!*—There are times when the saints have to stand before God, and receive into the depths of their heart his searching scrutiny (Mal. 3:1-3).

9-13. *Every beast of the forest is Mine!*—God holds the keys to the commissariat of the universe. Dost thou doubt that He can supply thy table?

15. *Call upon Me! . . . I will deliver.*—There is no uncertainty here. God knows our troubles; but He demands that we should *call.* Days of trouble are often sent to make us call.

21. *I kept silence.*—The silence of God in sight of the evil around is due to His longsuffering; but it will not continue forever (3).

23. *I will show the salvation of God.*—What a spectacle for

the holy soul! Our way may seem dark; but if we dare go on doing right, we shall certainly experience the Divine deliverance. Stand still, and see the salvation of God.

Psalm 51 "A BROKEN AND CONTRITE HEART"

There is no doubt as to the occasion or the authorship of this Psalm. It abounds with references to II Sam. 11 and 12. It is remarkable that such a confession should have been handed to the chief musician; but surely the publicity thus given to it has been a means of grace to all earnest worshippers in every age of the world. The repentance was as public as the guilt; and many a sin-stained penitent has trodden these well-worn steps, which bear the marks of pilgrims of all nations and lands.

What a story it is! "This saint of nearly fifty years of age—bound to God by ties which he rapturously felt and acknowledged, whose words have been the very breath of devotion for every devout heart—forgets his longings after righteousness; flings away the joys of Divine communion; darkens his soul; ends his prosperity; brings down upon his head for all his remaining years a cataract of calamites; and makes his name and his religion a target for the barbed sarcasms of each succeeding generation of scoffers. As man; as king; as soldier—he is found wanting. Why should we dwell on the wretched story, except that it teaches, as no other page in the history of God's Church does, that the alchemy of Divine love can extract sweet perfumes of penitence and praise out of the filth of sin?"*

1. *Thy loving-kindness . . . Thy tender mercies.*—Our only pleas for forgiveness are in God's loving kindness, and in the multitude of his tender mercies. It is only as we believe in these that we dare look at our sins. Nor can we ever forget that though the blood of Jesus did not purchase the love and mercy of God, yet it is only through his oblation and sacrifice that that love is able to have free scope in pursuing its tender office of redemption.

2. *Cleanse me from my sin!*—The plural *transgressions* (1) is

*Dr. Maclaren

here replaced by the singular *sin*, because all the successive crimes which had accumulated about his soul were branches from a common trunk. Mark these successive terms: *transgression*, the violation of law; *iniquity*, crookedness from the straight line of rectitude; *sin*, missing the mark.

3. *I acknowledge.*—However much God loves the penitent, and desires to forgive him, He dares not pardon until distinct confession has been made. Till then sin is like the fabled spirit of a murdered and unburied corpse—it is ever before the eye of the soul.

4. *Against Thee have I sinned.*—Every sin against man is still more a sin against God.

5. *I was shapen in iniquity.*—This was not said to extenuate, but to show how inveterate was the evil, needing infinite help and love.

7. *Purge me . . . wash me!*—How many are the expressions employed! *Blot out*, as from a record. *Wash*, as foul stains which must be rubbed and beaten out. *Cleanse*, as a leper: for whom the sprig of hyssop was always used (Lev. 14:4-9).

8. *Make me to hear joy!*—How gloriously bold to ask for restoration to JOY (12). Let us claim the music and dancing, as well as the best robe.

10-12. *A constant spirit* (marg.).—This is what we need to guard against future outbreaks—a *constant* spirit (*marg.*); God's *Holy* Spirit; and a *willing* spirit (R.V., *marg.*).

13. *I will teach transgressors.*—There is no such preacher as he who has been newly-forgiven. The forgiven Peter was the appointed preacher at Pentecost.

15. *Open Thou my lips!*—When God opens the lips, the devil and fear cannot shut them.

16, 17. *Thou desirest not sacrifice.*—Ceremonialism cannot free us from taint (Heb. 9:9-16). God's fire descends on broken hearts.

18, 19. *Do good unto Zion!*—When we are right with God, our sympathies and prayers overflow the narrow confines of selfish interest, and pour themselves out for the entire Church.

Psalm 52 THE DOOM OF THE EVIL DOER

The superscription fixes the occasion on which this Psalm was composed (I Sam. 22). It was at first suggested by Doeg's treachery; but it also had reference to Saul himself, to whom alone many of the allusions of the Psalm are applicable. And in after days this Psalm of David's wanderings was given to the chief musician for public use, because it contains, under the husk of a passing circumstance, the kernel of eternal truth.

1-4. THE TRAITOR'S SIN.—How safe are those who are entrenched in the favor of God! All else may pass, but that remains indestructibly the same. What terrible power there is in the tongue! (Jas. 3:4-11). A sharp razor, working deceitfully, will probably injure the hand that holds it.

5-7. THE TRAITOR'S FATE.—"Shall take thee away, and pluck thee," etc.; literally, "shall seize thee, and hurl thee away homeless (tentless, *comp.* Jer. 10:20). The outstanding idea is rejection of the impenitent by the Holy One. This is the ineveitable doom of sin. And one cannot but rejoice that the world has been so ordered as that wickedness meets its reward even here. The 7th verse contains the reflections of the righteous.

8. CONTRAST TO THE TRAITOR'S END—It is thought by some that Nob, where the tragedy took place, was situated on the Mount of Olives. If so, this allusion would be very appropriate. "As the olives grew all around the humble forest sanctuary, and were in some sort hallowed by the shrine which they encompassed, so the soul grows and is safe in loving fellowship with God." What a contrast between trusting in the abundance of riches, and in the mercy of God! The former take to themselves wings; the latter is forever (1). Oh to be among God's evergreens, drawing our supplies by roots struck deep down into Him, and trusting Him whatever betide!

9. The Psalmist's soul sings itself clear, and he determines to entrust his cause to God, and patiently await his vindication.

Psalm 53 WITHOUT GOD

A revision of Psalm 14. Twice is ATHEISM denounced in the Psalter. Line must be on line, precept on precept. *Mahalath* is "*sickness.*" Does not this Psalm lay bare the hereditary tendency of the heart of man to forsake God? In Psalm 14. *Elohim* is thrice used, *Jehovah* four times; here, *Elohim* is used throughout. There are some other differences:—

Psalm 14	Psalm 52
(1) Abominable works.	(1) Abominable iniquity.
(3) Gone aside.	(3) Gone back.
(5) God is in the generation of the righteous.	(5) God hath scattered the bones of him that encampeth against thee.

It is as if every effort were made to find more forcible expressions to describe the sin and the doom of those who deny God.

1. THE SEAT OF ATHEISM.—It is not in the head, but in the heart. And men keep on boasting of it, in the hope of making themselves believe it, and in order to keep their courage up.

2. THE ATTITUDE OF ATHEISM.—Its eyes are downward; if they were lifted for a moment, they would see God looking down.

3. THE UNIVERSALITY OF PRACTICAL ATHEISM.—Let each beware (Heb. 3:13).

2, 3. THE EVIL EFFECTS OF ATHEISM.—On the understanding and affection, so that corruption is bred through the entire nature (Rom. 3:10-17).

4. THE CRUELTY OF ATHEISM.—*Who eat up my people.* He who has no care for God is not likely to have much care for man. The prayerless man is an atheist in heart: "he calls not upon the Lord."

5. THE CAUSELESS FEARS OF ATHEISM.—How often have the enemies of God been seized with enexplicable panic! (Prov. 28:1; II Kings 7:6, 7.).

6. THE DIVINE ANSWER TO THE ATHEIST.—Even now the existence of God's ancient people is a marvellous reply to the taunts of his foes: but how dumb and silenced they will be when they see Israel restored as a nation, and when the saints shall possess the earth! *Oh that the salvation of Israel were come out*

of Zion! This is a prayer which befits every instance of depressed spiritual life.

Psalm 54 "GOD IS MY HELPER"

We are led by the superscription to I Sam. 23:19. The Psalm is short, as if compressed by the intensity of David's need. 1-3 contain a prayer for deliverance; 4-7 contain expression of confidence and praise. In the first he invokes the name of God; in the second he extols it. His trust throughout is in El, the Strong.

The Ziphites are described as strangers (3), though men of Judah like himself; because they were possessed of a spirit so contrary and alien to his own. It is rather beautiful to see how David refuses to say all the hard things which he might have said about Saul, and deals with those who enticed him into evil courses, as though he would cloke the sins of the Lord's anointed King.

1. *Save me, O God!*—A lonely, persecuted man, who has no other help, appeals from man to God, conscious of the rectitude of his cause.

3. *They have not set God before them.*—Not to have God before our eyes is to have them full of self-estimate, or of measurements after the standards of other men, uncorrected by thoughts of the claims of God's Holiness, Power, and Purity.

4. *Behold, God is my Helper!*—What faith is here! Hardly had the prayer ascended than the soul is aware of the gracious answer. Note this present tense: "God is mine helper." The eye sees nothing; but faith knows that the mountain is full of horses and chariots of fire. Saul sought David every day; but God delivered him not into Saul's hand. "The Lord is on my side" (Psa. 118:6; Rom. 8:31).

6. *With willinghood will I sacrifice;* or, "with free-will gift" (Exod. 25:2; 35:29). When God has saved us, let us yield ourselves to Him, as the woman in the Gospel yielded her alabaster box.

7. *He hath delivered me!*—When we pray in faith, we have the petition which we asked (I John 5:15). And when our

enemies are punished we have no feeling of vindictive satisfaction, but are thankful that God has vindicated his name and his truth.

Psalm 55 OH FOR WINGS LIKE A DOVE!

The groundwork of this Psalm was suggested by Absalom's rebellion and Ahithophel's treachery (II Sam. 15:12). But the Spirit leads out the Psalmist beyond the immediate occasion to depict the sufferings of our Lord at the hand of Judas. And the whole Church has fellowship with those sufferings, in the days of treacherous foes and false friends.

It may be divided thus: 1, 2, The cry of the soul; 3-8, A description of desperate need; 9-11, The sin of the city; 12-15, 19-21, A particularization of the plottings and deceit of a former friend; 16-18, Expressions of trust in God; 22, 23, Exhortations to others, founded on personal experience.

4, 5. *My heart is sore pained.*—How aptly do these words describe those deeply convicted of sin!

6. *Oh that I had wings like a dove!*—The dove is swift in its flight; and it ever hides before a storm. What a picture of timid innocence! How often do we suppose that we should find rest in changed circumstances! But the restless heart would be restless everywhere. The words of Jesus are the true answer to this cry for rest (Matt. 11:28, and Heb. 4:3).

12-14. *Thou . . . mine acquaintance!*—Our Lord, who bore his other sorrows in silence, exclaimed against the treachery of Judas, as if this were the drop which made His cup overflow.

15. *Quick*, i.e., *alive*, like Korah (Num. 16). Very different was the spirit of the old dispensation to that of Christ (Matt. 5: 43-45; 26:52; Luke 23:34).

17. *Evening, morning, and noon.*—Referring to the habit of the pious Jew (Dan. 6:10, 13). If we need to eat for physical strength thrice each day, do we not need to pray as often? But though we have our fixed times, no time is unreasonable. God's courts of appeal never rise, or close their doors.

22. *Thy burden,* as the margin (R.V.) suggests, is that which God has given thee to carry. "He cast it on thee: now cast it back

on Him." We cannot do God's work in the world, so long as we stoop under burdens which impede our energies; therefore hand over all, and let no burden be brought into the inner city to disturb its Sabbath-keeping (Neh. 13:19).

Psalm 56 "PUT MY TEARS IN THY BOTTLE!"

This Psalm was composed under the same circumstances as Psa. 34. Pursued by Saul, and almost in despair, David crossed the frontier, and took refuge in the city of Goliath. He was soon recognized, and resorted to the subterfuge of feigning himself mad (I Sam. 21). All the time he was acting thus, his soul seems to have been directing its eyes towards God. His faith was not strong enough to keep him from an unworthy disguise; but still faith was there. What a strange medley are we all at the best!—feigning madness in terror, and compiling psalms in heroic trust.

The Psalm falls into three strophes; 1-4; 4-11; and 12, 13. The earlier part of each of the two former describes the writer's danger; and the latter part in each case closes with a similar refrain (4; 10, 11).

The title is very touching, as the margin (R.V.) puts it; and perhaps there is a reference to Psa. 55:6.

3. *I will trust.*—We are reminded of I Sam. 21:12. It is better to say with Isaiah, "I will trust, and not be afraid" (Isa. 12:2). *See also* 4 and 11.

4. *I will not fear.*—Here for a moment the writer seems to have climbed out of the shadowed valley of fear to a mountain summit, sunlit. But in the next verse he is hurled back again. Oh to live, outside one's own experiences, in the unchanging Person and work of Christ! All praise and trust must be *in Him.*

8. *Put my tears into Thy bottle!*—No tear of the child of God falls unnoticed and forgotten. Remember how the sinner's tears were precious to the Master, whose feet they laved (Luke 7:38, 44). As rainbows are made of drops of water, so does God keep

our tears to transmute into songs. You will meet your tears again in rainbows (Isa. 61:7; Rev. 7:17; 21:4).

12. *Thy vows are upon me, O God!*—Vows had an important place in the Old Testament economy (Deut. 23:21-23; Ecc. 5: 4, 5): but the Sermon on the Mount (Matt. 5:33-35) seems to exclude them from the ethics of the new dispensation; though vows are twice mentioned in the Acts (18:18; 21:23): in both cases probably in connection with Nazarite consecration.

13. *My feet from falling!*—Here is a plea for those who have been saved from the penalty of sin, that their feet may be kept from falling. Oh to walk before God so as to please Him! (Gen. 17:1-8; Psa. 36:9).

Psalm 57 THE SOUL AMONG LIONS

This is one of the choicest of the Psalms. It is dated from the cave of Adullam or the hold at Engedi. The resemblances to Psa. 7 probably point to the latter. The Psalm falls into two parts, each of which closes with a similar refrain.

1. *In the shadow of Thy wings.*—As the hills were David's refuge from Saul, so was God the cave of refuge for his soul —being a safe hidingplace for us all. Is there not here also a reminiscence of words once spoken to the heart of his ancestress the Moabite maiden? (Ruth 2:12; *see also* Deut. 32:11). God's care is like an eagle's wing for strength, and like a hen's for gentleness (Matt. 23:37).

2. *God that performeth all things for me.*—Why should we not let God do "all things" for us and through us? (Heb. 13:20, 21).

3. *He shall send from heaven.*—With this confidence, we need not fear "him that would swallow us up."

4. *My soul is among lions.*—Delitzsch here says that, as the fugitive among those rocky fastnesses prepares himself for his night's rest, he hears the growl of the beasts of prey from which his refuge protects him; even so did God save David from his foes.

5. *Be Thou exalted, O God!*—Let us sometimes rise above our personal griefs in passionate desire for God's glory.

7. *O God, my heart is fixed!*—The steadfast and prepared heart is always in a condition of holy song. May God keep us fixed!

8, 9. *I will awake right early!* (R.V.,*marg.*)—If the earlier verses marked the writer's thoughts at eventide, here is his morning's resolution. *Glory* stands for *soul* (See also Psa. 16:9). He who lies down to sleep among lions shall yet arise to praise, and to set others praising.

10. *Be Thou exalted, O God!*—Mercy and Truth had come, as he expected (3; Psa. 36:5; 108:4). And, as he closes, he magnifies Him who stooping from above heaven had lifted him to heaven.

Psalm 58 "LIKE THE DEAF ADDER"

This Psalm is against wicked rulers. It has been suggested that it was written on account of Abner and the rest of Saul's princes, who judged David as a rebel and outlaw, and urged Saul to pursue him. It is the fourth of the Golden Psalms. For superscription, *see also* Psa. 57.

The divisions are very simple: a description of the evils of the unrighteous judges (1-5) ; prayer for their overthrow (6-8) ; the ultimate triumph of righteousness (9-11).

2. *Ye weigh out violence* (R.V.).—Weighing is always symbolical of JUSTICE; but these unrighteous judges weighed out *violence* rather than justice.

3. *They go astray as soon as born.*—It is said that the young serpent will sting as swiftly and as poisonously as an older one. And certain it is that the virulence of our nature will show itself in young children. Of course, by nature, we all share the fallen nature of Adam, though, in the case of the believer, grace neutralizes its effect.

4-5. *Like the poison of a serpent.*—The second clause may be rendered, *Like a deaf adder, he stoppeth the ear.* "The hearing of all the serpent tribes is very imperfect, as all are destitute of a tympanic cavity." The charmer has to reach the snake by very shrill notes of voice or flute. In the case of David's persecutors, it was not so much their inability as their unwillingness to hear.

Saul's conscience was not dead, for he was on more than one occasion touched by David's appeals (I Sam. 19:6; 24:17-21; 26:21, 25). But he resisted the prompting of his better self.

6. *Break their teeth!*—This imagery is borrowed from the lion, which tears his prey with his great eye-teeth.

7. *Let his arrows be as if they were cut*—headless, pointless, blunt, and harmless (Psa. 37:15).

9. Before the contents of the pots can feel the heat of the thorns burning beneath, God will take them away: both those which have not been reached by the fire, and are therefore green, and those which are burning. The rapidity and rush of the tempest, which sweeps away all preparation for the meal, is very vivid.

10, 11. Sooner or later the integrity of the righteous will be vindicated: and it will be manifest that the eye of the all-seeing Judge has discerned between the false and the true. There is a great distinction between the desire for the gratification of personal vengeance, and zeal for the vindication of God's character. Ah, what a commentary is supplied by Rev. 19:1-4!

Psalm 59 "DELIVER ME, O GOD!"

The fifth of the Golden Psalms. Compare the title with those of Psalms 16; 56; 57; and 58. Delitzsch says, "We believe that it is most advisable to adhere to the title." The contents of this Psalm correspond to the title, and carry us naturally to I Sam. 19:11.

It consists of four parts, of which the first and third are very similar: the second and fourth parts also resemble each other. *Compare* 1-5 with 11-13: also 6-10 with 14-17.

1, 2. *Deliver! defend! deliver! save!*—Four times the persecuted man cries for help. He speaks of his enemies as *workers of iniquity; men of blood; plot weavers; and insolent in their might.* How often must similar cries have been wrung from the Waldenses, the Huguenots, and the Covenanters!

3. *Transgression* rather refers to the treason with which David was charged against the king; *sin* as towards God. We should

habitually exercise ourselves to have consciences void of offence towards God and men (Acts 24:16).

4. *They run and prepare themselves.*—They made haste to manifest their enmity; yet their hatred was "without a cause" (Psa. 7:4; 35:7, 19; 109:3; 119:78, 161).

5. *Lord God of hosts, God of Israel.*—Dwell on these reduplicated names for God: *Jehovah,* the unchanging; *Elchim Sabaoth,* the God of hosts, indicating the resources at his command; *Elohe Israel,* the God of Israel, in his covenant relations. Each is a new plea, which God cannot resist (*see* also Jer. 35:17; 38:17).

6, 7. *Like a dog.*—The Eastern dog is a wretched animal, prowling through the streets to feed on offal, and filling the night air with howlings, when its search for food has been in vain. Thus for several successive nights David's foes may have gathered round his house, whispering, or pouring forth their hatred in muttered tones. Silence has settled on the houses all around, the inmates are wrapt in slumber: *Who doth hear?*

8. *Thou, O Lord, shalt laugh.*—What a bold image! God looks down through the dark, and laughs at them in scorn (Psa. 2:4).

9. *O my Strength, I will wait upon Thee* is the beautiful reading of the Revised Version.

10. *The God of my mercy.*—It might be read, "My God shall go before me with His mercy." Here is God's prevenient grace. He goes before the sheep which He puts forth: He marches in front to make the crooked straight, and the rough smooth (John 10:4).

11-13. *God ruleth unto the ends of the earth.*—These imprecations arise from fear lest his people should be hardened in sin.

16, 17. *I will sing in the morning.*—There is also here an amplification of David's former resolve (9). The morning is ever breaking on the godly, succeeding the night of anxiety and peril. Let it summon us to loud songs of praise!

Psalm 60 "SAVE WITH THY RIGHT HAND!"

This is a national Psalm to be *taught* to the people (Deut. 31:19). Verses 5-12 reappear in Psa. 108. As Psa. 13 was sung by the sons of Korah when the Edomites were taking advantage of

David's absence to invade the land, so this Psalm was composed after victory had been assured. *Shushan-eduth* means "the lily of testimony"; and may refer to the name of the tune to which this Psalm was set. *Aram* stands for the Syrians. The Syrians which dwelt between the two floods, Euphrates and Tigris, had become confederate with the Syrians of Zobah (II Sam. 10:6, 8, 16, 19). For the whole story, see II Sam. 8.

The nation's anguish (1-4); the nation's confidence in God's word (5-8); the nation's prayer (9-12).

1. *Thou hast been displeased.*—These earlier verses have a plaintive tone, due to the great losses inflicted on the land by the Syrian invasion. Sometimes disasters fall so thick on the Church that it seems as if it were God-forsaken.

4. *Thou hast given a banner.*—There is the more reason for claiming God's help, because his people carry the banner of his truth. If it is trailed on the ground, great dishonor is done to his holy name.

5. *Thy beloved.*—We are "beloved" indeed, if we are in the Beloved (Deut. 33:12; Eph. 1:6).

6. *I will divide . . . and mete out.*—This is an allusion to God's promise that His people should possess Canaan (Gen. 12:7, etc.) And therefore the nation rejoices in its certain victory over its foes. When we have any promise of God, we may confidently depend upon it.

Shechem and Succoth are described as contiguous in Gen. 33:17, 18. As it was promised in Jacob's days, so should it be (Gen. 28:13-15; 35:11, 12). The enemy should not succeed in wresting an inch from Israel.

7. *Gilead is Mine!*—Gilead, though lying across the Jordan, should not be dismembered. Manasseh and Ephraim, the martial tribes, and Judah, the seat of government, were welded into a strong united kingdom, and should remain so.

8. *Moab . . . Edom . . . Philistia.*—The three hereditary foes of Israel had been reduced to subjection. Moab, a washing tub (II Sam. 8:2); Edom, a slave taking care of sandals (Matt. 3:11), or the idea may be of the transference of authority (Ruth

4:7); Philistia, compelled to welcome with shouts of triumph (Psa. 108:9).

9. *Who will lead me?*—The victor pants for new victories. The *strong city* is probably Petra, the famous capital of Edom, hewn in rock.

11, 12. *Give us help!*—The cry for help and the assurance of deliverance go hand in hand. Here is a motto for us in all times of opposition and difficulty.

Psalm 61 "THE ROCK THAT IS HIGHER THAN I"

Neginah implies that the Psalm was intended for singing to instruments. It was evidently composed while the tabernacle was standing (4); and after David had received the promise of the everlasting kingdom (6, 7). Yet he was manifestly passing through a time of great distress; and Delitzsch is, therefore, probably right in fixing its date at the time of Absalom's rebellion, and in heading it, "Prayer and Thanksgiving of an expelled king on his way back to his throne." It is a precious gem.

1. *My prayer.*—How earnest it is!—*my cry!*

2. *The end of the earth* is any place of extreme sorrow or depression; it is equivalent to the *uttermost* of which Heb. 7:25 speaks. We are never really far off from God; but, owing to depression, and physical weakness, and the oppression of our foes, we may feel ourselves to be so. But we are never too far off to cry to Him.

My Rock!—What rock is this, save the Rock of Ages, cleft for us? And yet we cannot climb up into its clefts: we need the hand of Divine grace to lift us thither, and keep us there. "I will put thee" (Exod. 33:22).

3. *A shelter! . . . a strong tower!*—What God has been, He will be.

4. *In Thy tabernacle forever.*—If permitted to return. David purposed to abide forever in the sacred shrine. But everywhere God pitches a pavilion for us. These are the outspread wings of the shechinah (Psa. 36:7). Ah, what a heritage is here! (Eph. 1:3).

6, 7. *His years as many generations.*—Words which can only be fulfilled in their entire wealth of meaning in the King of kings.

8. *I will sing praise* (Psa. 5:3; Phil. 4:6).

Psalm 62 "MY SOUL WAITETH UPON GOD!"

This is the "only" Psalm (*see* verses 2, 4, 5, 6). It consists of three strophes, each of which begins with that word *only* or surely, *ach* in the Hebrew (1-4; 5-8; 9-12). The first two divisions (1-4; 5-8) close with "Selah." This Psalm was probably composed during the time of Absalom's rebellion; and it resembles Psa. 39 in being dedicated to Jeduthun (I Chron. 25:1-3); and that Psalm also gives the Hebrew word *ach* four times: it is there translated *surely* and *verily.*

1. *Only my soul waiteth,* or "is silent unto."—There are times when words fail us, and when the soul mutely waits for God's salvation. Silence is often golden eloquence, and God can understand it. Moreover waiting on God stills the soul.

2, 6. *I shall not be moved.*—The movement is only on the surface of the life, while the great deeps of the soul are at rest (Acts 20:24).

3. *How long?*—It is probably David who was the bowing wall and tottering fence (*see* R.V.). One thrust, and his enemies think he will be at their feet.

5. *My expectation.*—It is well for us if we have learned to look away from all creature-help to God alone.

6. *My rock! my salvation!*—What a loving accumulation of endearing titles for God! The man of fifty catches up the imagery of earlier years, and ransacks memory to supply fit names for this Almighty Friend. And all that God is, is *mine.*

8. *At all times,* means on dark as well as bright days. When the heart is charged with sorrow or sin, what a relief it is to open the sluice gates, and pour all out toward God!

9. *Lighter than vanity* (*see* R.V.): They go up as the lighter scale, lighter than vanity, *i.e.,* a breath. How often have we looked for help from men and money in vain!—but God has never failed us.

10. *Oppression . . . robbery.*—The men of high degree oppress; the men of low degree are fraudulent: but the evil deeds of both are seen and known of Jehovah. The increase of riches has its dangers: it generally means the increase of temptations.

11, 12. Power and Mercy are the two pillars on which the Temple of His justice rests.

12. God is neither unseeing nor unmindful (Psa. 10:14; Heb. 6:10).

Psalm 63 "MY SOUL THIRSTETH!"

This is said to have been from the third century the morning song of the Church. The superscription tells us that it was written in the wilderness of Judah. But the word "king" (11) forbids our supposing that the Psalm was penned during the Sauline persecution. It was probably written amid the events recorded in II Sam. 15:23-28; 16:2; 17:16. This "wilderness" stretched southwards from Jericho on the western shore of the Dead Sea. In the Psalm there are noticeable references to the life of the soul. *My soul thirsteth; my soul longeth; my soul shall be satisfied; my soul followeth hard after Thee* (1, 5, 8).

1. *Early will I seek Thee!*—This should be the cry of each of us in the dawn of life, and of each day: "In a dry and *weary* land" (R.V.). How weary and sad is life without God! Though we have all, yet if He be not there, our soul is athirst and weary (John 4:13, 14).

2. *To see . . . as I have seen Thee!*—As the Psalmist trod sadly over the burning sand, and crossed the dry torrent-beds, it seemed a picture of his state of soul; and he contrasted the present with the happy past, when he had had similar desires, which were then slaked by the vision of the Divine power and glory.

3. *Thy loving-kindness is better than life.*—Already a sense of the love of God breaks on his soul, as a tropical rain on the parched earth; and he becomes assured of speedy satisfaction.

5. *As with marrow and fatness.*—God not only gives us necessaries but dainties.

6. *In the night-watches.*—Many of David's most rapturous

experiences of God seem to have been at night. In all these Psalms there is imagery borrowed from the night-watch in the camp.

8. *Thy right hand upholdeth.*—The hand of God ever supports the soul in its pursuit of Him (Phil. 3:12).

9. *Those that seek my soul.*—Perhaps there is an allusion here to Num. 16:31, 32.

10. *A portion for foxes.*—Absalom's army was badly routed, and many of the slain must have fed the jackals which roamed the forest (II Sam. 18:6-8).

11. *Shall rejoice in God.*—"By Him," refers of course, not to the king, but to God.

Psalm 64 THE COUNSEL OF THE WICKED

This Psalm probably dates from the Sauline persecutions. The slanders of the tongue, specially mentioned, are very characteristic of that period. There are two strophes: prayer for preservation (1-6), and assurance of Divine vindication (7-10).

1-5. *Hide me from . . . the wicked!*—What a marvellous picture is given here of the whole range of calumny! Insult, sarcasm, slander, inuendos, tale-bearing, and suspicion are rife enough in our society, and even in Christian society. How fond are we all of hearing and spreading reports of which we have not taken the trouble to ascertain the truth! Sometimes it is a look, or a gesture, or a shrug of the shoulders; but it may be enough to ruin a man's reputation.

6. *They search out iniquities.*—If this search is always on foot, how careful and circumspect should we be! (I Cor. 10:32).

7-9. *All men shall fear.*—God relieves us of the necessity of fighting for ourselves. Whilst the wicked are bending their bows against us (3), God's arrow is flying from an unsuspected quarter against them. Curses come home to roost (8).

10. *The righteous: the upright.*—The Psalm began with the singular ("*my* voice": "hide *me!*") and ends with the plural. Our experiences enrich the whole Church. And those who trust shall have abundant cause for rejoicing and praise.

Psalm 65 THE RIVER OF GOD

This joyous hymn was probably composed for use in the sanctuary on the occasion of one of the great annual festivals. It expressly dwells on the Divine bounty in the fertility of the earth (Lev. 23:9-14). There is a marvelous blending of nature and grace in its entire texture, which makes it one of the most beautiful of all sacred lyrics.

There are three divisions. We are transported successively to the Courts of the Lord's house (1-4); to the shore of the sea, where rockbound coasts resist the fury of the waves (5-8); and to the pasture-lands and cornfields of Canaan (9-13.)

1. *For Thee is the silence of praise* is the literal reading. Such praise as is too great and deep for tumultuous expressions, and so arrests the fever of the soul. It has been said, "The most intense feeling is the most calm, being condensed by repression."

2. *Unto Thee shall all flesh come!*—By the word *flesh* the Psalmist would call attention to our weakness and need as men (Gen. 9:11, 15; 136:25; Isa. 40:5), each deficiency on our part pointing us to God. The more needy we are, the greater cause is there for going to God. And He answers prayer. There is no definition of the kind of prayer which He answers, because the outward expression matters nothing, if the heart speak. And wherever the heart speaks, God hears.

3. *Words of iniquities* (marg.).—This prevailing may be because they act more masterfully, or because they excite deeper contrition. The Hebrew word *capher* translated *cover* implies, "to cover with the atonement." And the pronoun, *Thou,* is emphatic, intimating that God, and God alone, could do this.

4. *Blessed is the man whom Thou choosest.*—God hath chosen Christ and all who are one with Him (Eph. 1:4). We need to be *caused,* ere we can approach or dwell (John 6:44; Gal. 4:9). But in each case God is prepared to do this by the Holy Spirit. *Dwell in Thy courts.* What a sacred position would this be! Why should we not seek it! "And go no more out!" (Rev. 3:12). *Satisfied.* Such a condition is involved in the realization of the presence of God, and when we are abiding in Him. *Thy holy*

temple. The word "temple" was applied to the Lord's house even before Solomon's temple was eretced (I Sam. 1:9; II Sam. 22:7).

5. *By terrible things in righteousness.*—The terror is towards God's foes; the answer towards his friends (II Sam. 7:23). Ultimately all mankind shall come to acknowledge Him (Isa. 66: 16, 18). *Afar off upon the sea* will mean not only those afloat, but those living on the seashore, in distant lands.

8. *The morning and evening* may mean dwellers in East and West; or the mercies which characterize dawn and eve, and which lead us to new songs and joys.

9. *Thou visitest the earth.*—Every spring is like a Divine visit. The holy soul looks through second causes to the present tenses of the I AM.

10. *Thou waterest the ridges.*—The ridges of the ploughed fields are lowered through the plenteous rains, and fertilized to fatness.

12, 13. *The hills rejoice; the pastures are clothed; the valleys are covered.*—Let us seek an equal fertility in the life of the soul, through that river of God, which is the Holy Spirit (Rev. 22:1).

Psalm 66 "VERILY GOD HATH HEARD!"

Some of the old expositors speak of this Psalm as the Lord's Prayer of the Old Testament. It consists of five divisions (1-4, 5-7, 8-12, 13-15, 16-20), of which the second and the fifth begin in a similar manner—*Come ye!*

1. *All ye lands!*—Notice the missionary spirit which breaks through the narrow limits of Judaism. Thus are men larger than their creeds. *See also* 4.

2. *Make His praise glorious!*—We should make our praise as worthy of its object as possible. Praise Him with a glorious hymn!

3. *How terrible are Thy works!*—God's manifested power will only make his enemies yield a feigned obedience. See *marg.*, R.V. Grace alone can change their hearts.

5. *Come and see!*—Thus Jesus spake, and Philip (John 1: 39, 46).

6. *Through the Flood!*—The Red Sea and the Jordan. Is not this always true of the Church, that God's people are passing through obstacles which must daunt them, were it not for their Divine companion (Isa. 43:2). Our God turns the place of trial into one of joy. "Isa. 11:11-15 leads us to anticipate a repetition of the miracle of the divided waters."

7. *His eyes behold the nations.*—The metaphor here is of God looking forth on men from his heavenly watch-tower with eyes that carry with them the light by which they see.

10. *Thou hast tried us!*—"It is not known what corn will yield, till it come to the flail; nor what grapes, till they come to the press. Grace is hid in nature, as sweet water in rose-leaves. The fire of affliction fetcheth it out." Satan tempts us to our fall and ruin; God tries us to show what grace He has implanted, and to strengthen them by exercise.

11, 12. *Thou broughtest us into! . . . Thou broughtest us out!*—The Psalmist sees God's will, not only in his appointments, but also in his permissions. He is said to do what He permits to be done. The imagery is of beasts, first netted; then heavily laden (the *loins* being the seat of strength); then driven by men who almost sit over their heads, dominating them as they choose.

12. *Through fire and through water.*—Fire and water were used in purifying the spoils of war (Num. 31:23). We need something more than water (Matt. 3:2). He who brings us into the trial will certainly bring us out. The wealthy place is a well-watered place (*see marg.*); the word is translated in Psa. 23:5, "runneth over."

14. *Opened lips* (marg.) are probably mentioned to show that the vows were made under strong internal pressure which forced the lips open.

16. *Come and hear!*—These words befitted the woman of Samaria, and the Gadarene demoniac (John 4:29; Mark 5:19, 20); and they suggest the duty of all those who have received special help and blessing.

17. *I cried unto Him.*—Scarcely had I cried, than I had reason to praise.

18. *If I had regarded* (R.V., marg.).—Be sure that you are on God's errands, and not on some sinful or selfish quest.

20. *God hath not turned away His mercy.*—We have no plea in prayer, like God's mercy.

Psalm 67 "LET THE PEOPLE PRAISE THEE!"

This Psalm was probably composed, like Psa. 65, to be used at one of the great annual festivals, probably the Feast of Tabernacles. The singer goes beyond the occasion which called forth his song, and seems to include in the range of his thought those spiritual blessings which accrue to all the world through the Gospel of Jesus Christ.

1, 2. *Cause His face to shine!*—There is an allusion here to the threefold blessing of Num. 6:24-26. When Abraham and his seed are blessed, the world is blessed through them. Similarly we may plead that God would bless his Church and people as the condition of blessing to the world. Oh for the shining of that dear face, undimmed by any cloud born of our sin and neglect!

3. *Let the people praise Thee!*—We want crowns for the brow of Christ. Each loyal heart yearns for the exaltation of its King.

4. *Thou shalt judge . . . and govern.*—To govern is to *lead* or *tend* (see *marg.*). Christ shall yet be the Shepherd of mankind.

6. *The earth hath yielded her increase* (R.V.) as if already the Millennial age had broken on the rapt gaze of the poet-prophet, and all the harmonies of nature were restored. Praise ever accompanies the fertility of the Church. *Our own God.* What rapture there is here! Faith lays its hand on God, and appropriates Him for itself. There is a wide difference between speaking of things and people as fair and useful, and saying of them, "These are my own." He is *our own,* because He has made Himself so, and has taken us to be his forever. "His every act pure blessing is."

Psalm 68 "LET GOD ARISE!"

This Psalm is one of the grandest odes in existence. It was probably composed when the Ark was brought up in triumph by the united people (27) from the house of Obed-edom to the newly-acquired Mount Zion (II Sam. 6). It is evidently a processional hymn, to be sung by multitudes of white-robed priests and Levites; and we may almost mark the successive divisions of the melody as corresponding to the several stages of the march.

Whilst the Ark is being lifted to the shoulders of the Levites, a measured strain is chanted (1-6); as the procession then moves forward, the march through the wilderness is recited (7-14): presently Mount Zion comes in sight, and all neighboring hills are depicted as looking askance and enviously at its selection in preference to themselves (15, 16); the procession now begins to climb the sacred slopes of Zion amid more triumphant strains (17, 18): the procession is next described (19-27); and from the assembled hosts, now gathered on the sacred site, the strains of triumph peal forth (28-35).

1. *Let God arise!*—These opening words were the formula used by Moses (Num. 10:35). How strange their history! "Through the battle smoke of how many a field have they rung! On the plains of the Palatinate, from the lips of Cromwell's Ironsides; and from the poor peasants that went to death on many a bleak moor to their rude chant;—

"'Let God arise, and scattered
Let all his en'mies be;
And let all those that do Him hate
Before His presence flee.'"

4. *Cast up a highway for Him that rideth through the deserts* (R.V.).—As the Ark of God once led his people through the wilderness, so now does the Word of God ever lead us through dark and difficult places.

5, 6. *Setteth the solitary in families.*—God has a special care for lonely people; and in his providence He often introduces such into the warmth and fellowship of family life (*comp.* John 19:26, 27). *He bringeth out the prisoners into prosperity* (R.V.).

9. *A plentiful rain.*—"A rain of liberalities," probably referring to the abundant gifts of every kind bestowed on the people.

11. *The women that publish the tidings are a great host* (R.V.); an allusion to the Oriental custom of damsels celebrating a victory in song and dance. How marvellously this is being fulfilled now by the exodus of noble girls from their happy homes to publish to the heathen the Gospel of Jesus!

13. *Covered with silver.*—The Authorised Version gives good sense, contrasting the blackening contact of a smoky caldron with the lustrous colors flashed from the dove's wing.

14. *White as snow.*—"Salmon" means *shady, dark.* It was a high mountain near the Jordan. The kings were scattered, as snowflakes are driven before the wind, and melt before the sun.

15. *The hill of Bashan.*—Bashan is the high snow-summit of Hermon. It is employed as a symbol of worldly greatness. But the lesser Zion is as great—and greater, since God is there. God does not choose the great and strong of this world (I Cor. 1:26).

18. *Gifts for men.*—"Thou hast obtained spoil which Thou mayest distribute as gifts among men." Thus the Holy Spirit gives the exact sense, though not the words, in Eph. 4:8.

19. *Who daily beareth our burden* (R.V.).—Either rendering (A.V. or R.V.) is delightfully suggestive.

22. *I will bring again my people.*—Though the danger be as great as that caused by Og in Bashan, or by the passage of the Red Sea, yet will God deliver his people.

27. *Benjamin, with the princes of Judah.*—The union of the tribes at the extreme North and South is emblematic of the union of the Church of the ascended Lord (Eph. 4.).

30. *Rebuke the wild beast of the reeds* (R.V.). referring to Egypt, as representing heathendom.

31. *Ethiopia shall stretch out her hands.*—A glimpse of days not far away.

Psalm 69 IN DEEP WATERS

This is the second Psalm with this title, "Upon the lilies" (*see* Psa. 45.). It touches the profoundest depths of sorrow, which were only fully known and trodden by our blessed Lord. Of course, there was a primary reference to the sorrows of the Psalmist; but only in Jesus is there a full realization of much that is here expressed. Clearly, however, the maledictions with which wrong-doing is threatened had no place in Him, who from his cross asked his Father to forgive. This, like Psa. 22., is constantly applied to Christ in the New Testament. *Compare* 4, with John 15:25; 9, with John 2:17, and Rom. 15:3; 21, with Matt. 27:34, 48; 25, with Acts 1:20.

4. *Without a cause.*—The last clause is a proverbial way of saying, "I am held guilty of wrongs, which I have never done," as when Shimei charged David with Saul's sins (II Sam. 16:8).

8. *A stranger unto my brethren.*—True of David (I Sam. 17:28), and of our Lord (John 1:11; 7:5).

9. *Reproaches are fallen upon me.*—All these foregoing verses may serve to show us how deep and agonizing was the travail of the Redeemer's soul, when He came to his own, but they received Him not, and accounted Him a winebibber and sinner.

13-21. *There was none to pity.*—Read these verses once or twice, and think into them some of the meaning with which Jesus uttered them. It is probable that He literally died of a broken heart—this was evidenced in the blood and water of John 19:34.

22-28. *Let them be blotted out.*—That such will be the fate of the wicked is undeniable; but though the saint foresee it, he will not desire it for selfish reasons.

35. *Thy holy places.*—We began with "deep mire where there was no standing": we end in the abiding city of God.

Psalm 70 "I AM POOR AND NEEDY"

This Psalm reminds us of Psa. 40. Indeed, it is a repetition of its closing verses. It was composed as a Psalm of remembrance, to put God in remembrance of his suffering ones. "When God seems to forget us, we must not forget to put Him in remembrance" (Isa. 43: 26; 62; 62:6, 7, *marg.*).

1. *Make haste to deliver!*—God often delays to come to our help, and tarries till the fourth watch of the morning, or the

night before the execution; but He is never too late. Yet we often chafe at the delay.

2, 3. *Put to confusion.*—Wicked spirits as well as men seek after our soul; but God shall turn them backward and disappoint their designs.

4. *Let God be magnified.*—How much better to *say*: "Let God be magnified," than, "Aha, Aha." The godly man boasts in God, and is only eager that his name should be exalted (Phil. 1:20). Let it be our one aim to do and suffer all with this one purpose—to make all men think better of the great God.

5. *Poor and needy.*—Happy are they who have learned to glory in their infirmities, and to use them as arguments with God. There is a beautiful answer to this plea in that description of the Messiah which is given in a following Psalm (82:4): *Helper* in good works; *Deliverer* from all the power of the adversary.

The prayer closes with one further plea for urgency.

Psalm 71 FOR DECLINING YEARS

The writer and the occasion of this Psalm are unknown. It is obviously an old man's psalm (9, 17, 18). The divisions fall naturally into prayer (1-13), and the expression of confident hope (14-24). The three first verses are a reproduction with slight variations of Psa. 31:1-3. One key-note is *Great* and *Greatly* (19, 20, 21, 23). Another is *All the day* (8, 15, 24).

2. *Incline Thine ear unto me.*—If you are too weak to cry aloud, God will stoop to you.

3. *My strong habitation.*—How approachable is God at all times! There is a door at St. Peter's which is opened only once in a century; but God's door stands always open.

5. *Thou art my hope.*—Not only is our hope in God, but God is our hope. Not created things; the Creator alone can satisfy us. "Christ is in us, the Hope of Glory."

6. *My praise shall be continually of Thee.*— Let us praise God for his mercy in his ordinary works, and have eyes for his daily miracles.

9. *Cast me not off in the time of old age.*—*Compare* Josh. 14:10-14. Our weakness is a prevalent and irresistible plea.

14. *I will hope continually.*—The strain changes from prayer to hope.

15. *My mouth shall praise.*—How soon has the answer come to his petition! (8).

16. *In the strength of the Lord God.*— The Septuagint translates "I will enter into the powers (mightinesses) of the Lord," as into a sure citadel. But there is great force and beauty in our version.

17. Thou hast taught me.—Be content to let God teach you just one step or lesson at a time. And declare what you are taught.

21. *Turn again and comfort me* (R.V.).

22. *Thou Holy One of Israel.*—This name for God occurs only in two other Psalms (78:41, and 89:18). My God cast the dumb devil out of us, and set us talking on this theme, which can never become threadbare!

Psalm 72 THE COMING KING

Critics insist that *for* in the inscription should be *of*; and that therefore this glorious Messianic Psalm was composed by Solomon. A conclusion which is not contradicted by verse 20, which was evidently appended (with the Doxology) by those who divided the Psalter into books, the second of which closes with this glowing description of the Lord's Anointed and his reign. Behold the kingdom of heaven which is already set up, and shall come yet more and more!

1. *Give the King thy judgments.*—This reminds us of I Kings 3:9-28. In all judging and advising we need to catch sight of that which is in God's mind, and to reproduce it. This is what the Holy Spirit did for our Lord, and will do for us (Isa. 11:2-4). How instantly this petition was answered! (*see* the next verse).

3. *Peace to the people.*—Peace as the result of righteousness (Isa. 32:17; Heb. 7:2). It was, and still is, common in the East to announce great events from the tops of the mountains (Isa. 40:9).

4, 5. *He shall judge the poor.*—Compassion for the poor makes the throne endure. But how infinitely true this is of our Lord, to whom so many of these expressions must apply! (Rev. 5:9).

6. *Like rain upon the mown grass.*—The *mown* grass is that which is shorn. On the shorn blades, suffering still from the scythe, that gentle rain descends which heals and revives: emblem of the blessed work of the Holy Spirit.

7. *Till the moon be no more* (R.V.).

8. *The river*—the Euphrates (Exod. 23:31; Deut. 11:24).

10. *The kings of Seba shall offer gifts.*—Tarshish, on the far West, by the Straits of Gibraltar; Sheba and Seba, nations in South Arabia famed for their wealth. "The most *uncivilized*—the most *distant*—the most *opulent*—shall pay homage to Christ."

11. *All kings . . . shall serve Him.*—Kings of wealth, and thought, and music, and art, have already acknowledged Him, and shall (Rev. 19:16).

12. *The needy . . . when he crieth.*—Our needs are arguments and reasons with Christ.

15. *Prayer for Him . . . continually.*—"Men shall pray for Him continually: they shall bless Him all the day long" (R.V.). "We pray for Christ," says Augustine, "when we pray for the Church of Christ; because it is his body." We pray for Him when we say, "Thy kingdom come!" Though Christ is King of the poor, He shall have abundance of gold.

16. *An handful of corn in the earth.*—Though there be but a handful, yet such shall be the marvellous increase that the slopes of the mountains shall wave with corn as Lebanon with cedars. As there is abundant produce in the country, there shall be vast populations in the city, numerous as blades of grass.

17. *His name shall have issue* (R.V., *marg.*).—It shall reproduce itself. The Gospel of the name of Jesus begets children in every nation enlightened by the sun. Well for us if we claim those blessings which are in Him for us (Eph. 1:3).

18-20. *Blessed be the Lord God!*—This doxology reminds us of Psa. 41:13, where the first book is closed. It is a sublime aspiration, in which we, who see the beginnings of this beneficent reign, may well unite.

Psalm 73 "SET IN SLIPPERY PLACES"

This and the ten following psalms are ascribed to the family of Asaph, the eminent singer (I Chron. 16:7; II Chron. 29:30). The author describes his conflict with a strong temptation to envy the wicked. The 37th Psalm, as well as the 73rd, discusses this problem, which was the great stumbling-block of the saints of old.

We may divide the Psalm thus: How he came into the temptation (1-14); how he got out of it (15-20); how he profited by it (21-28).

1. *Truly God is good!*—This is the great principle on which he stands, as on a slab of granite. "Only good is God" (R.V., *marg.*). Whatever appearances there may be to the contrary, there is no doubt as to His perfect beneficence. The Israel is not after the flesh, but after the Spirit (John 1:47; I Cor. 10:18). If you are washed in the blood of Christ, believe that every wind which blows on your life comes from the quarter of God's love.

2. *My feet were almost gone.*—Almost, but not altogether.

4. *No bands in their death.*—This might be rendered, "no pangs up to their death" (R.V., *marg.*), or it may mean, that their death is easier than that of the godly. Their life flows on in a softly flowing current. "Men may die like lambs; and yet have their place hereafter with the goats."

6-9. *They are corrupt.*—What a picture! Their haughty bearing; their eyes and their speech; the imaginations of their evil heart overflowing (7, R.V.). They blaspheme God in heaven, and wander through the earth in search of garbage.

10, 11. *How doth God know?*—Some think that these verses indicate that the perplexity of the saints, coupled with the baleful influence of the wicked make the Lord's people apostatize; others, that we here told of the anguish caused them by the tyranny of the proud oppressor.

13, 14. *Chastened every morning.*—These verses might be paraphrased thus: "Surely godliness does not profit. I have lived up to all I knew to be right, keeping my conscience void of offence; and yet plagues and chastisement have been my daily lot.

Is there a God, or is He other than good, that He so deals with his most faithful servants?" "Plagued" (*contrast* verse 5).

15, 16. *Too painful for me.*—It seems treacherous to breathe such thoughts about God; and yet it is an infinite pain to doubt God's perfect integrity. Ah, the agony of a suspicion that God should not be perfectly wise and good!

17-19. *Until I went into the sanctuary.*—Let us view things from God's standpoint, and take in the whole course of his providence, weighing the future retribution of the wicked against their present estate (James 5: 11).

20. *As a dream.*—"The awaking of God is a metaphor for his ending a period of probation or indulgence by an act of judgment": and here it would seem that death, which separates a man from his prosperity, is specially referred to.

21, 22. *So foolish was I.*—When a man is nearest God, he is most full of self-loathing. God forgives him; but he cannot forgive himself.

23-28. *God is . . . my portion forever.*—In spite of all the follies and sins of the past and present we may have God's constant presence; and in Him we can have all and more than all that the Godless find in their wealth. God in heaven; God in the pathway of daily life; God in the heart—this is blessedness.

Psalm 74 "WHY HAST THOU CAST US OFF?"

This Psalm was composed when the Chaldeans destroyed the temple and city (*compare* verse 8 with Jer. 52:13-17). The Psalmist describes his people's miseries (1-11); recounts the reasons why they should still trust in God (12-17); and concludes with urgent petitions for help (18-23).

3. *Lift up thy feet*, i.e., come not slowly, but quickly, to restore ruins which otherwise must be perpetual.

4. *Thine enemies roar.*—The shout of the foe breaks in on the holy calm of congregations gathered for solemn worship; and heathen standards wave over the buildings consecrated to God.

5. *They seemed as men that lifted up axes upon a thicket of trees* (R.V.).

8. *They have burned the synagogues.*—As early as Samuel's time there were meetings on fixed days for worship (I Sam. 9:12; 10:5). And these were probably maintained by the prophets (II Kings 4:23), and anticipated the synagogues of later times.

13, 14. *Dragons in the waters—Leviathan.*—These monsters stand here for the Egyptian hosts.

15. *The fountain and the flood.*—The Chaldaic adds to the Jordan, the Arnon, and the Jabbok (Num. 21:13-15).

16, 17. *The day is thine, the night also.*—Our God is the God of nature. What can He not do? The night may be overshadowing your life; but it is as much his as the day: and there are treasures in darkness (Isa. 45:3).

18. *Arise, O God!*—It is blessed to feel that God's glory and our deliverance are indentical (verse 22).

19. *Thy turtle dove.*—What a striking similitude for the Church in its simplicity, weakness, and defencelessness!

20. *Have respect unto the covenant.*—There is no stronger plea with God than this: for the "covenant" is ordered in all things and sure (II Sam. 23:5).

This Psalm may be recited by the saints in all times of the Church's depression.

Psalm 75 "HE PUTTETH DOWN AND LIFTETH UP"

It is fitting that the wail of the previous Psalm should break forth into glad thanksgivings of this. This title resembles that of Psa. 57., *Destroy not*: and probably this triumphal ode was prepared to celebrate a deliverance of which faith was sure. Reference is probably made to Sennacherib's invasion in the time of Hezekiah (Psa. 46; 76.). The *north* is therefore omitted, as one of the quarters from which help would come (6); it was thence that the invader came.

1. *Thy name is near.*—The believing soul gives thanks before the blessing of deliverance has come to hand. Its ear is quick to detect the *pibroch* of the relieving force, though the cannonade of the foe is fiercer than ever.

2. *I will judge uprightly.*—This is the reply of Jehovah,

while his people are yet speaking (Isa. 65:24). "When I shall find the set time" (R.V.) *i.e.*, when the set time has come.

3. *I bear up the pillars of the earth.*—What a comfort it is to feel that amid the chaos and anarchy which sweep the surface, God is holding fast the solid foundations, on which we may build without fear!

4, 5. *Lift not up the horn.*—The Psalmist here becomes the speaker. The *horn* is the strength of certain beasts, and is the symbol of power (Deut. 33:17; I Sam. 2:1-10); and often of the power of the ungodly (Dan. 7:7). The word occurs four times in this Psalm; and it appears in some other Psalms.

6. *Neither from east, west, nor south.*—*Promotion* stands for deliverance—the lifting up of God's help.

7, 8. *A cup . . . the dregs thereof shall the wicked drink.*—God's judgments stupefy by their suddenness and terror (Rev. 16:18-21).

10. *The righteous shall be exalted.*—The prophets are sometimes said to do things in which God is evidently the Agent (Jer. 1:10). This is emphatically the Psalm of the second Advent.

Psalm 76 "THOU ART TO BE FEARED"

If the former Psalm anticipated Sennacherib's overthrow, *this* was written after it (3, and Isa. 37).

2. *In Salem is his tabernacle.*—Salem was the ancient name of Jerusalem, and signifies Peace. God can only dwell where there is peace (Acts 2:1). The dwelling-place of God is among his people.

3. *The shield, the sword, and the battle.*—God snaps the proudest instruments of war.

4. *More glorious than mountains.*—The world-kingdoms are compared to mountains covered with spoils; but the city of God is fairer than the best.

5, 6. *Cast into a deep sleep.*—God did but speak a word, and the warriors of the king of Assyria slept their last sleep. The poet depicts the scene in the camp on the morning after the dread catastrophe:

> The eyes of the sleepers waxed deadly and chill,
> And their hearts but once heaved, and forever were still.

9. *God arose to judgment.*—God sometimes seems to sit and allow matters to take their course: but He is waiting for the set moment to interpose; and when He arise, as He ever will, on the behalf of his people, the earth is still, as nature before a thunderstorm.

10. *The wrath of man shall praise Thee.*—What is meant in malice is changed to blessing. And there is a limit beyond which the rage of the enemies of the righteous cannot pass (Job 1:12; I Cor. 10:13).

11. *Vow and pay* (II Chron. 32:22, 23).—*See* Note on Psa. 56:12.

12. *He shall cut off . . . princes.*—"Cut off" as a vinedresser would cut off shoots. The spirit, *i.e.*, the life of princes (Rev. 6: 15; 14:18, 19). How terrible must be the wrath of the Lamb, to those who have defied and resisted his love!

Psalm 77 "THE WATERS SAW THEE"

This Psalm is still ascribed to Asaph, but it is after the manner of Jeduthun (inscription, R.V.). There are resemblances to it in Hab. 3:8-15, so it was probably composed before the end of Josiah's reign, in which Habakkuk lived. The carrying away of the ten tribes and the imminent captivity of Judah may have furnished the occasion of this sad lament.

We may divide at the Selahs.

1-3. *I cried with my voice* EXPRESSES THE PSALMIST'S ANGUISH.—How often do we need the day of trouble to make us seek the Lord! The passage, "my sore," etc., is better rendered, "my hand was stretched out" (R.V.). This refusing to be comforted recals Gen. 37:35 and Jer. 31:15. What excessive grief is here!

4-9. *I am so troubled that I cannot speak.*—A CONTRAST BETWEEN PAST AND PRESENT.—In this scarcity of comfort, Trapp says that the Psalmist was glad to live upon his old stores, as bees in winter. Particularly he remembered his song in the night (Job 35:10), which is equivalent to that "glory in tribulation" of which the New Testament is full (Rom. 5:3; II Cor. 7:4). It is wholesome to compare the present with the past, so that we may repent if we are conscious of any backsliding; and that we may be led again to the feet of Christ.

After long days of gloom and anguish have darkened the soul, it begins to fear lest it may never emerge from the darksome forest into the open. Melancholy and depression are apt at putting questions; but faith has ever an answer ready.

"Will the Lord cast off?" *No!* (Rom. 11:1.)

"Will He be favorable no more?" *His compassions fail not!* (Lam. 3:22.)

"Is his mercy clean gone forever?" *No!* (Psa. 103:17)

"Does his promise fail?" *No!* (Heb. 6:18.)

"Has God forgotten to be gracious?" *No!* (Exod. 34:6.)

"Has He in anger shut up his mercies?" *No!* (Psa. 103:17.)

10-15. *I will remember.*—FAITH RESTORED BY MEMORY.—The years of God's past love are not likely to be all in vain. Has He loved from eternity, and will He forsake or forget in time? God's way is in the sanctuary, *i.e.*, it is holy (13); but it is also in the sea, *i.e.*, it is full of mystery (19) "Some providences, like Hebrew words, must be read backwards."

16-19. A POETICAL ACCOUNT OF THE PASSAGE OF THE RED SEA. —The thunderstorm here described is almost implied in Exod. 14:24. God does as He will: but no difficulties are obstacles to Him; and, what He has done, He can do. He still speaks to the waves (Mark 4:39).

20. *By the hand of Moses and Aaron.*—"Great was the power of these two men; but neither was the shepherd of the sheep: each was a servant of the Great and Good Shepherd, who made use of their hands."

Psalm 78 GOD'S DEALINGS WITH ISRAEL

This Psalm specially refers to the children of Ephraim, as representing the northern kingdom of Israel (9, 67); and is intended to show the cause of their rejection, and to warn them against incurring further judgments. It may date from II Chron. 13. Is not Asaph a type of our Lord, who is ever thus pleading with his Church?

Divide thus: A call for attention (1-8); the story of Israel's many rebellious and providential deliverances in the wilderness (9-39); the narrative is continued to their settlement in the land of Canaan (40-55); the reason for and the fact of the transference of leadership from Ephraim to Judah (56-72).

9. *Ephraim . . . turned back.*—During the time of Ephraim's headship, the nation failed at the gates of Canaan to go forward to take the land: hence the transference of leadership.

12. *In the land of Egypt.*—Zoan, or Tanis, was a very ancient city on the Nile, the capital of a district (43).

20. *Can He give bread also?*—What faithless hearts are ours! God has filled heaven and earth with proofs of his love, and yet we distrust Him. "Oh, slow of heart!" (Mark 8:18.)

21, 22. *Because they believed not.*—Nothing so grieves and angers God as unbelief.

32-42. *How oft did they provoke Him!*—An epitome of the forty years' wanderings.

43-51. *He wrought his signs in Egypt.*—Several additional descriptive touches are here given to the account of the plagues.

49. *Evil angels.*—Not evil spirits, but agents of suffering and pain.

50. *He made a path for his anger* (R.V.), *i.e.*, He did not restrain it.

59-61. *He forsook the tabernacle of Shiloh* (*see* I Sam. 4:11).

66. *He smote his adversaries backward* (R.V.).

72. *So He fed them . . . and guided them.* Sincerity of purpose and tact in handling men are essential to a true ruler and guide.

Psalm 79 "WHERE IS THEIR GOD?"

This Psalm, like Psa. 74., evidently dates from the Chaldean invasion. In Psa. 74. the destruction of the Temple was the prominent thought; here—its defilement is deplored. There are three stanzas; narrative (1-4); prayer, especially because God's name and glory are at stake (5-12); promises of perpetual praise (13).

1. *The heathen are come into Thine inheritance.*—In other passages God Himself is described as the chief agent. Here we find specified the tools employed by Him (Exek. 5:11; 23:38).
2, 3. *Blood . . . shed like water.*—Fulfilled II Chron. 36:17; Zech. 14.; *see also* Rev. 11:7. The words of these two verses are said to have been constantly on the lips of our countrymen in the days of the Indian Mutiny.

5. *Jealousy . . . like fire.*—Jealousy is the reverse side of love. Jehovah was a husband to his people; hence his severity (Amos 3:2). We should be very particular as to our walk, lest we cause bitter heart-pain to the Lover of souls (I Cor. 10:22).

6. *Pour out Thy wrath.—Pour out* is the same word as is translated *shed* in ver 3. This verse is quoted by Jeremiah (10: 25).

8. *The iniquities of our forefathers* (R.V. (Deut. 5:9).—Let us ask God to remember, in his dealings with us, not the sins of our past, but the covenant which He made with our fathers.

9. *Help us, O God, for the glory of thy name.*— We have an irresistible argument when we plead for God's glory (John 14:13).

10. *Let the revenging of the blood of thy servants be known* (R.V.)—Joel quotes the former clause (2:17).

11. *Let the sighing of the prisoner come before Thee!*—The answer is anticipated in Psa. 102:19, 20.

13. *We will give Thee thanks forever.*—In pastures of never-failing bliss, we shall give Him perpetual praise (Rev. 7:17).

Psalm 80 "A VINE OUT OF EGYPT"

Under the figure of a vine injured by a wild beast (8-13) the Psalmist laments the degradation of the ten tribes. The house of Joseph always represents Israel, as distinct from Judah (Obad. 18; Amos 6:6). The mention of Benjamin (2) does not militate against this view; for though the southern part of the tribe clung to the fortunes of Judah, it is probable that the bulk of the northern portion followed those of the ten tribes to whom they were bound by many ties (Gen. 43: 29). These three tribes marched together (Num. 10:22-24). The title of the Psalm reminds us of 45 and 69. "Lilies" are an emblem of what is lovely, and here of the lovely salvation of God.

The division is clearly marked by the recurrence of the refrain (*Turn*), 3, 7, 14 (R.V.), and 19. The name of God being on an ascending scale: God (3); God of Hosts (7, 14); Jehovah, God of Hosts (19).

1. *Shepherd of Israel.*—In Jacob's blessing of Joseph, this title is specially given to God (Gen. 49:24). To sit enthroned upon the cherubim (*see* R.V.) is an emblem of omnipotence, for they represent all creatures. Thus the gentleness of a shepherd and the almighty power of God blend in this verse.

2. *Before Ephraim, and Benjamin, and Manasseh, i.e.*, at their head, as the pillar of cloud and fire led the wilderenss march.

3. *Turn us again.*—What a prayer for a backslider! (Jer. 31: 18). When God restores us He puts us back into the very place which we occupied before we fell.

4. *How long wilt Thou be angry?* (*smoke,* R.V.)—Not the fire of God consuming the sacrifice of God, but burning against the backslider (Psa. 74:1).

5. *Bread of tears.*—Bread composed of tears (Psa. 42:3).

8. *A vine out of Egypt.*—Another ıeference to Jacob's prediction, "A fruitful bough" (Gen. 49:22). The point of the Psalmist's reference to the past consists in this—that God cannot desert, or destroy, any work which He has once begun.

10, 11. *The hills*—those of the southern boundary of Canaan; *the cedars* represent Lebanon and the extreme north; *the sea* is the Mediterranean; *the river*, the Euphrates.

12. *All they . . . do pluck her.*—Pul; Tiglath-pileser; Sargon and others (II Kings 15:19; I Chron. 5:26; II Kings 18:11).

15. *The branch* (*lit.* "the son," as verse 17) is another term for the spiritual vine; and in the allusion to the right hand (15, 17), there is surely a reference to the name which Jacob gave to

Benjamin, "Son of my right hand" (Gen. 35.18). The name was given by the father under Divine inspiration, and was a pledge of Divine love, not only to him, but to the whole nation whom he represented.

17. *The Son of Man.*—Surely our Lord alone perfectly fulfils this description. He is that Son of Man, whom God has made strong for Himself. And God's hand is pledged to maintain Him until the ravages of Satan are made good, and the vine of his church covers the land.

18. *So will we not go back.*—We are redeemed, that we should not go back to our old sins, but show forth the praise of our Deliverer.

Psalm 81 "MY PEOPLE WOULD NOT HEARKEN"

Probably written by Asaph himself, in the days of David, this Psalm is a call to the people to keep the Passover, the annual feast commemorating the deliverance of Egypt.

Division—A call to celebrate the Passover (1-3); the basis on which the Passover rests (4-7); an appeal to Israel to come back from false gods to their allegiance (8-12); with a promise of the blessings which may yet accrue to them (13-16).

1. *Sing aloud unto God!*—We can sing aloud unto Him when we realize the great blessings which He is prepared to confer on us, as the remaining verses of this Psalm disclose. Think much of God's resources, all of which are yours in Christ; and then praise Him.

3. *The new moon* or month may probably mean the first and chief month of the year, the Passover month, the month of Abib (Exod. 12:1, 2: Deut. 16:1). *The time appointed* is "the set time." Hengstenberg considers that the whole Psalm refers to the commemoration of the Passover: "our solemn feast day."

5. *This He ordained in Joseph.*—Joseph is mentioned here as representing Israel, because his position in Egypt constituted him the leader amongst his people. We should never forget our deliverance from a more intolerable servitude; but commemorate it —specially in the Lord's Supper. The change to the first pronoun

indicates how closely the Divine Spirit was behind the Psalmist, so that most naturally, and with no break in the continuity of thought, he passes from one mode of address to another.

6. *I removed his shoulder from the burden.*—"His hands were set free from the burdenbaskets." Such baskets were found in the sepulchral vaults of Thebes, and were doubltless used in carrying from one place to another the clay and manufactured bricks. Our Saviour has done more than this, relieving us from care and burden-bearing (Matt. 11:28; Psa. 55:22), admitting us into glorious liberty.

7. *In the secret place of thunder.*—God was supposed specially to reside in the storm cloud. Thence He looked on the hosts of Pharaoh, and spoke from the brow of Sinai. We are reminded of that triplet of Lowell's:—

> Behind the dim unknown
> Standeth God within the shadow,
> Keeping watch above his own.

8, 9. *Hear, O My people!*—What a peculiar claim God has on the whole-hearted allegiance and devotion of his own! Let us each time that we are tempted to desert Him, recall the cost at which He has redeemed us.

10. *Open thy mouth wide!*—God wants our emptiness: He calls on us to open our mouth, even as the gaping beak of the young fledgling. There is nothing which we really need that He is unable or unwilling to supply. Let us ask Him to fill us with the Holy Ghost, and reckon that He does keep his word (Eph. 5:18).

12. *They walked in their own counsels.*—"With the froward Thou wilt show thyself froward" (II Sam. 22:27; Psa. 18:26; *see also* Rom. 1:24; II Thess. 2:10, 11).

13. *Oh that My people had hearkened!*—Obedience is the condition of full deliverance. Note the stress laid upon "hearing" and "hearkening" (8, 11, 13).

14, 15. *The haters of the Lord.*—Our enemies and God's haters are indentical. What encouragement is here! Notice also the permanence of our standing: "for ever."

16. *With the finest of the wheat.*—Strength and sweetness; necessaries and luxuries; complete satisfaction!

Psalm 82 "THE POOR AND NEEDY"

The Psalm of the magistrate; perhaps composed on the appointment of judges by Jehoshaphat (II Chron. 19:5-7). There is an admonishment for past misconduct (2-4); followed by a lamentation over their obduracy, and a declaration of their doom (5-7). Luther says, "Every prince should get the whole Psalm painted upon the walls of his room; for here such will find what high, princely, noble virtue their situation demands, so that assuredly worldly supremacy, next to the office of the ministry, is the highest service of God and the most profitable duty upon earth." A very interesting and close parallel to this Psalm occurs in Isa. 3:13-15.

1. *God judgeth among the gods.*—Some think that the word "gods" refers to angels; but this will not suit the tenor of the Psalm. The word unquestionably stands for *magistrates and judges.* In Exod. 22:28, the people were taught to recognize in governors the reflections of the authority of God. Their judgment was said to be God's (Deut. 1:17); and whoever came before them, came before God (Exod. 21: 6). There could be no doubt, then, that the Heavenly Judge would call them to his bar, if they grossly misrepresented Him.

2. *How long will ye judge unjustly?—Compare* Lev. 19:15.

5. *They walk on in darkness.*—In spite of Divine protests, men will take their own way. With their back to the true light, they go on towards a darkness which grows denser at every step.

6. *Ye are gods.*—It seems at first strange that men so wicked should be dignified by so high a title. But that appellation rather records God's ideal of their sacred office, and calls them to fulfil it. Our Lord quotes this verse in arguing with the Jews (John 10:34); his point being that, if Scripture calls unjust judges "gods," because they filled the place and represented the majesty of God, surely his opponents had no right to accuse Him of blasphemy, because, as "the Sent of God," and engaged in doing his Father's will, He also spoke of Himself as God.

7. *Like one of the princes.*—If man is lifted to high office, he is but man still. His office, but not his nature, is God-like. And if

he do wickedly, he must fall as other princes have fallen before him.

8. *Arise, O God!*—This call to God to undertake the judgment of the world is like the cry of the Church to her absent Lord, that He would make haste to right the wrongs of time, and to bring in his glorious kingdom (Rev. 6:10)

Psalm 83 "BE NOT STILL, O GOD!"

This Psalm was composed on the occasion described in II Chron. 22. In that chapter we are told distinctly that the Spirit of the Lord came on Jahaziel, of the sons of Asaph (verse 14). Perhaps he was the author of this Psalm. This was a song of praise sung before the battle, in sure anticipation of victory.

A short prayer for help (1), is followed by a description of the agony of the people which drove them to take refuge in their Divine Deliverer; the doings (2-4) and the numbers (5-8) of their foes. And then, reminding God of what He had done in the days that were past, the singer entreats Him to do the same again, establishing his glory in an incontestable manner (9-18).

2. *Thine enemies.*—It is a great source of courage, when we can feel that those who attack us are also in conflict against God; and that God takes our side against our foes and sins.

3. *Hidden ones* (I Kings 19:18; Psa. 31:20; Matt. 23:37; Col. 3:3).—If only we keep under the covert of God's wings, how safe we are!

4. *Let us cut them off!*—It is a daring attempt indeed, when men deliberately set themselves to annul God's eternal purpose. "The stars in their courses" (Jud. 5:20) fight against all such. There was great wisdom in Gamaliel's counsel (Acts 5:39).

5-8. *Confederate against Thee.*—A great confederacy with one fell purpose. Men who are naturally enemies to each other are allies when they can injure God's people.

9-12. *Sisera, Oreb, Zalmunna.*—Three deliverances of the past are quoted as specimens of the help which the land required (Jud. 4, 5, 7, 8).

13. *Like a wheel!*—"The wheel" is rather "the whirl." And the whole is equivalent to "as the stubble." which is whirled round and carried away.

14. *As fire on the mountains.*—The bracken or furze on the mountains is a ready fuel for the lightning spark which sets it ablaze.

16-18. *Let them be put to shame!*—The disasters which are imprecated on the allied forces are intended to lead them to recognize the supremacy of God. But there is no need to attempt to show the consistency of these petitions with the spirit of Christ: they are evidently inspired by the spirit of that older dispensation, which our Lord so distinctly set aside, as the husk from which the grain has passed into new and more perfect development (Matt. 5:38, 39).

Psalm 84 "A DAY IN THY COURTS"

One of the sweetest of the Psalms. The Gittith is said to have been a musical instrument on which some of the Psalms were played. The speaker is evidently the anointed king (9), a title which clearly designates David, who constantly uses it of himself. The conception of this sacred poem must have been his during the exile caused by Absalom's rebellion, even though its elaboration and ultimate form may have been due to the sons of Korah. Psalms 42 and 43 are inseparably connected with this in their plan and structure; in the coloring of their language; and in their rare and beautiful figures. *See also* Psa. 27:4.

The first *seven* verses, divided into *four* and *three* (as is often the case in the Psalms), contain a meditation; the remaining *five* are a prayer. Note the three *Blesseds* (4, 5, 12).

1. *How amiable are thy tabernacles!*— *Amiable* in the sense of *beloved.*

2. *For the living God!*—The longing and fainting are closely joined with rejoicing—for so might *crieth out* be rendered (*see* R.V., *marg.*): and therefore they do not indicate the pain of unsatisfied desire, but of desire which is immediately satisfied, though it still craves for more. The soul which has enjoyed most of God's

grace longs most earnestly for it; and in proportion to its longing is its joy.

3. *The sparrow hath found an house.*—This does not mean simply that he envies the birds which build in Zion; but that he himself is as a sparrow or swallow, which, after long wandering, has found a home and nest in God's house. "My poor little soul, the terrified little bird, has now found its right house and nest, even thine altars. If I had not found this, I must have been as a lone bird on the house-top, or an owl in the desert." Notice that it is in the altar that rest is found, *i.e.*, in the life of consecration and obedience. If you can say, "My King," you have found your nest.

4. *Blessed are they that dwell in thy house.*—Though not literally, yet spiritually, we may dwell in the Lord's house all our days (Psa. 23:6; 27:4). As long as you are able to praise, you are there.

5. *Whose strength . . . whose heart.*—Two conditions of blessedness: to have God as your strength, and to have in your heart ways. Too many hearts are full of cliffs and precipices; but they need levelling, so that there should be a highway for God (Isa. 40:3, 4.).

6. *The valley of Baca* is the valley of tears. Some speak of it as the valley of tear-shrubs. But there the righteous will find wells of salvation. If you are now in the valley of tears, be sure you are on the way to the city, and look out for the wells.

10. *A doorkeeper in God's house.*—Better be Lazarus at the threshold of God's house, than Dives in his palace.

11. *A Sun and Shield.*—A Sun in dark hours, and a Shade in scorching ones. Grace is the bud of glory; glory the flower of grace. If God has given the first, He will give the second. If He withholds aught on which you have set your heart, believe it is not really good; and still trust Him. We stand in grace and look for glory (Rom. 5:1, 2.).

Psalm 85 "MERCY AND TRUTH"

There is no clue to the historical associations of this Psalm. The description of the distress through which the nation had been passing is quite general. It will, therefore befit all times of anxiety and depression.

We have first a description in *seven* verses of the long-protracted misery of the people; and in the *six* remaining verses the strong expression of confidence of help and deliverance.

1-3. *Thou hast forgiven . . . iniquity.*— The Psalmist recounts a former instance of God's gracious intervention; and in this he sets us an example which we may well follow. Our captivity may continue long; but it will be brought back. Iniquity may be aggravated; but it can be forgiven. And the forgiveness of God will cover sin, as the deluge the highest mountains. There is probably an allusion here (3) to Exod. 32:12: "turn from thy fierce wrath."

5. *Wilt Thou be angry forever?*—God's anger is short-lived where there is contrition ("For a moment" Psa. 30:5).

6. *Revive us again.*—Spiritual revival is the indispensable condition of quickening and rejoicing.

8. *He will speak peace.*—God ever "speaks peace" to his saints, though the world is in revolt (John 20:19-21). Note the recurring references to righteousness and peace (Heb. 7:2).

10. *Mercy and truth are met.*—Mercy and righteousness are on one side; truth and peace on the other. They seem going on different errands and in different directions. But they meet at the cross of Jesus. There we have "the bridal of the earth and sky" (Isa. 45:8).

12. *The Lord shall give good.*—God gives nought but good; and all good is from God (Jas. 1:17).

13. *Righteousness shall go before Him.*—Righteousness not only looked down from heaven; but, in the person of Jesus, it has trod our earth, leaving footprints for us to follow (I Pet. 2:21).

Psalm 86 "BOW DOWN THINE EAR!"

David is in straits, deprived of human aid, his life endangered by a band of proud and ungodly men. And he quotes the help given him by God in former days (13). Obviously, then, this must refer to his sufferings at the hand of Absalom and his advisers.

The Psalm is divided into two strophes. The first ten verses make up the first, and the remaining ones the second. Notice the refrain in 5, 10, 15, "Thou art good!" "Thou art great!" "Thou art God alone!" Thou art full of compassion!"

1, 2. *I am poor and needy!*—He founds his prayer on his misery, and on the fact of his being one of God's chosen ones. "I am holy" might be rendered "I am godly" (R.V.). The Creator is the best Preserver. And He who has begotten passionate desires after Himself can best meet and satisfy them.

4. *Rejoice the soul of thy servant.*—"We may expect comfort *from* God when we maintain communion *with* God. God's goodness appears in two things, in giving and forgiving. We may expect that God will meet us with his mercies when we in our prayers send forth our souls to meet Him."

11. *Unite my heart to fear thy name.*—Our thoughts are apt to wander and scatter. We therefore need so much that God would gather them up into a true unity (Phil. 3:13, 14). The united heart, which has but one purpose and desire to live for God, is the heart which is most sure of God's "way," and most full of praise (12); and that experiences most fully His delivering care (13).

15. *Full of compassion.*—Who can fathom the fullness of God's compassion? (Rom. 11:33; Eph. 3:19; Phil. 4. 7).

16. *Give thy strength unto thy servant.*—Well is it when we come to the end of our strength, and begin to appropriate God's (Phil. 4:13).

Psalm 87 THE GATES OF ZION

This is a song of praise for some great deliverance; and from end to end it is full of triumphant joy. It seems to have dated from the times of Hezekiah, when Babylon was still second in power to Rahab (Egypt). *Rahab* means haughtiness or pride, and is used by Isaiah sarcastically (30:7, R.V.). "I have called her

[Egypt] *Rahab that sitteth still.*" "Rahab" (that is *Pride* or *Arrogance*) could only be applicable to Egypt before the battle of Carchemish (II Chron. 35:20-24), which humbled that nation's pride. The appellation "Rahab" is also found in Psa. 89:10 and Isa. 51:9. It seems clear that this Psalm (87) celebrates the security of Jerusalem after the discomfiture of Assyria by the angel of the Lord.

1. *His foundation is in the holy mountains.*—The foundations of Zion were laid in the eternal choice and determination of God. And those of the Church rest on the chief Corner-stone, our blessed Lord (Isa. 28:16). "Holy" surely means "set apart" from ordinary and common use. All is holy which is set apart for God.

2. *The gates of Zion.*—Are you quite sure that you are safe inside through faith in Jesus?

3. *Glorious things are spoken of Thee.*—What glorious things have been spoken of the people of God! They are a chosen generation, a royal priesthood, a holy nation, a people for a possession (I Pet. 2:9); the body and bride of Christ (Eph. 5:25). To be where Jesus is, at the right hand of God—*this* its destiny.

4. *I will mention Rahab and Babylon as among them that know Me* (R.V.).—In those days, when the numbers of the chosen people were much reduced, the heart of the Psalmist yearned with peculiar eagerness for the ingathering of the nations, according to ancient promise. There is also here an anticpation of the new birth, which makes different nationalities one family in Jesus Christ.

5, 6. *When He writeth up the people.*—There is a reference here to citizen-rolls (Luke 2:3). Whole hosts of nations are even now tracing all that is best in them to the religion which emanated from Mount Zion; and the time is coming when the forces of the Gentiles shall literally return to that city, which is to be the metropolis of a redeemed and rejoicing world (Isa. 60:11).

7. *Singers and players on instruments.*—The mention of singers and dancers (R.V.) summons to our thought the idea of a triumphal procession like that of Israel after the passage of the Red Sea. "All my fresh springs," as the Prayer-Book version has

it (*see also* Psa. 84:6; Isa. 12:3). Would that we were more content to be channels through which those springs might visit the world! (John 7:38).

Psalm 88 "INCLINE THINE EAR!"

This and the following Psalm constitute a pair. They were probably written during the reign of Zedekiah, but before the Captivity. The nation stood on the brink of a precipice; but the city and temple had not as yet been destroyed. *Mahalath Leannoth* means "the distress of oppression." It is a Psalm to give instruction to all sufferers as how to bear the griefs which lie heavily upon them. Stier says of this Psalm: "It is the most mournful of all the plaintive Psalms; yea, so wholly plaintive, without any ground of hope, that nothing like it is found in the whole Scriptures." Hengstenberg says: "The fact is all the more striking, that the Psalm begins with the words, 'O Lord God of my salvation,' after which the darkness grows continually thicker to the close." Surely in its deepest meaning, this Psalm is applicable only to the Prince of Sufferers.

1. *O Lord God of my Salvation!*—In the greatest griefs, it is much to be able to say "God of my salvation." Say it, if you do not feel it: you will come to feel it.

2, 13. *Unto Thee have I cried.*—In this dark hour the writer still feels that there is hope in God (Psa. 42; 43): and that prayer is the true resource of the overburdened spirit.

3. *Full of troubles.*—O troubled soul, others have trod your path. See the "blazed" trees along the track. You may be sure that this is the way to the reward.

6. *In the lowest pit.*—If we are willing to lie in the grave with Christ, we shall share His resurrection (Phil. 3:10).

8. *Mine acquaintance far from me* (John 8:16; 16:32).

9. *I have called daily upon Thee.*—There are times when prayer seems unavailing; yet must we keep on praying. So has it ever been (Matt. 15:25).

14. *Why hidest Thou thy face?*—God does not give his reasons.

What He does, we know not now, though we shall know (John 13:7).

18. *Lover and friend . . . far from me.*—All forsook the Man of Sorrows and fled. He knew what loneliness meant. But no ledge of rock along which He leads his own is too narrow for Him to go beside them (Isa. 63:9).

Psalm 89 THE LORD'S MERCIES

This is the other side of our experience, contrasted with that set forth in the previous Psalm. As the two sides of our earth, the one in darkness, the other illuminated. This Psalm especially records God's faithfulness (1, 2, 5, 8, 24, 33). And though there is a touch of the old melancholy, especially towards the close, yet on the whole the Psalm rings with a happier tone, and glistens with the sparkle of hope.

First, there is a remembrance of God's promise which secured the perpetual existence of David's kingdom (1-37); then a complaint that the present condition of affairs is in sad contrast to all this (38-45); last, a prayer that God would interpose (46-51).

2. *Mercy shall be built up forever.*—Mercy is a structure never done, layer on layer, storey on storey, tier on tier. God's *faithfulness* is as sure as the heavens (*see also* Psa. 36:5; 57:10; 108:4).

3, 4. *A covenant with my chosen.*—Supply, "For Thou didst say" (II Sam. 7:8-16). In troublous times we must cling to God's promises.

5-14. *The heavens and the earth are thine* (*see also* Psa. 19:1, 2; 77:16).—Full of praises, from heaven and earth; from angels, men, and nature.

15-18. *The people that know the joyful sound.*—The blessedness of the believer (*see also* Psa. 1;32:2; 40:4; 112:1).

19-37. *Established forever, as the moon.*—An exquisite description of the rise and development of David's power, which was a shadow of Christ's. As the sun and moon change not, but remain faithful to their posts in the heavens, so God's covenant is unalterable, made with Christ and all who believe in Him.

38-51. *Remember, Lord!*—In this plea for mercy we may well

join, on the behalf not only of Israel, but of the Church; not only because of the insolence of our foes, but because of the dishonor done to the name of God. But even in the midst of all this sorrow, the Psalmist is able to grasp deliverance; and so the Third Book of the Psalms ends in the light of an ascription of praise (52).

Psalm 90 "THREESCORE YEARS AND TEN"

There is every reason to accept the superscription of this Psalm as correct. It was written by Moses at the close of the forty years' wanderings; and perhaps about the same time as his other two songs (Deut. 32 and 33). If so, it was old when Homer sang. The imagery is all borrowed from the desert march: the desert streams, which soon dry; the night-watch in the camp; the short-lived growth of the grass before it is blasted by the "khamsin," or desert wind (5). The melancholy strain is due to the incessant funerals and the aimlessness of the desert marchings.

1. *Thou hast been our dwelling-place.*—God is our Home. Let us live in Him. Satan cannot enter to drag us forth (I John 4:16).

2. *From everlasting . . . Thou art God.—Earth,* our planet; *World,* the universe. God is above all change, because He lives in the eternal ages. There never was a period in which Jehovah was not. He is more permanent than the most changeless things.

3. *Thou turnest man to destruction.*—In opposition to the eternity of God is the transitory life of men. It seems long to us when we compare it with our days; but how short, when compared with the eternity of Him who looks on a thousand years as a brief night-watch! (II Peter 3:8).

4. *A thousand years . . . are but as yesterday.*—"As to a very rich man a thousand sovereigns are as one penny; so, to the eternal God, a thousand years are as one day."—Bengel.

7. *By thy wrath are we troubled.*—Moses now ascends from the melancholy fact of the brevity of life to the melancholy cause, that it is due to the wrath of God incured by our sins (*compare* Gen. 2:17; Rom. 5:12).

8. *Our secret sins.*—Does not this teach us that there are sins so secret that none but God detects them? But his eyes carry the light by which they see (Rev. 1:14). What a comfort to turn to the blood of Christ which cleanseth from all sin!

9. *As a tale that is told.*—"As a sigh" (R.V., *marg.*). This description is true of the unsaved and rebellious: but of believers we have a gladder description (I Cor. 6:11).

11. *The power of thine anger.*—God's wrath, which abides (John 3:36) on those who refuse to believe, is worse than those who have feared it most have ever conceived of it.

12. *So teach us to number our days.*—We should reckon our shortening days, and work harder, as the poor sempstress whose last candle is burning low (John 9:4).

14. *Satisfy us early!*—"Early" in life, and each morning, too: "Oh, satisfy us in the morning with Thy mercy" (R.V.).

16, 17. *Thy work; thy glory; thy beauty.*—All these blend in Jesus. And, as we abide in Him—his deeds are done through us; his glory shines around us; his beauty adorns us (Psa. 27:4).

Psalm 91 "THE SECRET PLACE OF THE MOST HIGH"

This Psalm is entirely general. But it is of great service to travellers, and to all who are exposed to danger and hardship. It alternates between the expressions of personal trust and exhortations to trust: hence the interchange of the pronouns "I" and "Thou." It is attributed by the old Rabbis to Moses, and indeed corresponds to his experience on the night of the first Passover. Satan quoted verses 11 and 12 to our Lord (Matt. 4:6).

1, 2. We may regard verse 2, 'I will say of the Lord, He is my Refuge," etc., as the soliloquy of the man described in verse 1, "He that dwelleth in the secret place of the Most High, and abideth under the shadow of the Almighty."

3. *Surely He shall deliver thee.*—Deliverance from guile and traps, as well as from the insidious pestilence of jungle and morass.

4. *Under his wings shalt thou trust.*—The wings of God! (Deut. 32:11, 12; Matt. 23:37).

5, 6. *Thou shalt not be afraid.*—In each verse we have the alternations of day and night, for there is not an hour which has not its special liabilities of harm. The soldier gets a dare-devil courage from the motto: "Every bullet has its billet." The believer flinches not, because his life is "hid with Christ in God" (Col. 3:3).

9. *Thou hast made the Lord . . . thy habitation.*—There must be definite appropriation on our part before there can be deliverance.

11. *He shall give his angels charge over thee.*—Do we make enough of the gentle, careful ministry of the angels? (Heb. 1:14; Luke 22:43). But certainly we must be in God's ways, ere we can claim angel-help.

13. *Thou shalt tread upon the lion and adder.*—This reminds one of some marvellous words of our Lord (Luke 10:19, 20), and surely refers to our spiritual foes (Mark 16:18; I Cor. 15:26).

15. *I will be with him in trouble.*—It is worth our while to be in trouble, to have such a Companion. He is never so near as then.

Psalm 92 "IT IS A GOOD THING TO GIVE THANKS"

This Psalm was intended for use in the public worship of God upon the Sabbath; on which day, according to Lev. 23:3, there was held a holy convocation. The Psalm is well fitted for its purpose, for on such a day men ought to find leisure to consider the works of God, and to praise Him. One theme for lasting praise is God's preservation of his Church in the midst of a hostile world.

2, 3. *To show forth thy loving-kindness . . . and thy faithfulness.*—Perhaps at the morning and evening sacrifice. What themes for morning and evening worship!

4. *Thou, Lord, hast made me glad.*—Let us learn to joy in God Himself (Rom. 5:11; 11:33). But especially on his own day let us remember the work of the Redeemer, which has made us glad for evermore.

5-8. *Thy thoughts are very deep.*—God so often delays the punishment of the wicked, owing to reasons hidden from our sight. His ways are very deep to the eye of man.

10. *Like an Unicorn.*—The wild ox or buffalo (Num. 23:22; Deut. 33:17). Thou enablest me to rise up with spirit, with a sense of strength, in an attitude of attack. The fresh anointing should be sought every morning (I John 2:27).

12-15. *The righteous shall flourish like the palm tree.*—In God's trees, the strength of grace does not fail with the strength of nature. But on the contrary, the Apostle Paul witnesses in II Cor. 4:16.

Psalm 93 "THE LORD REIGNETH!"

It is thought that this Psalm dates from the Assyrian invasion, and that it is the might of the terrible Assyrian foes which is here compared to the mighty breakers of the sea (R.V.) But the Psalm well befits all times of anxiety and opposition, and it is interesting to remember that this, and the six Psalms which follow, have always been applied by the Jews to the days of the Messiah. Surely then we may apply them to the Lord Jesus.

1. *The Lord reigneth.*—It is a great support to know that above and beyond all that here hinders and distresses us, there exists the great fact of Jehovah's sovereignty. This encourages us in conflict; this sustains us in the hour of trial. Five times in Scripture is this declaration repeated (I Chron. 16. 31; Psa. 93:1; 96:10; 97:1; 99:1; Rev. 19:6). This is also the war-cry of the Church in answer to the defiance of her foes. Calvin says: "All acknowledge with the mouth what the prophet here teaches; but how few place this shield in front of the might of the world, so that they fear nothing, be it ever so terrible." Thus might we oppose all attacks of our spiritual foes, and find ourselves ever victorious. What a magnificent apparel—majesty and strength!

3. *The floods have lifted up their voice.*—The sea is the usual symbol of the tumultuous masses of the nations. In this splendid reiteration, we can almost hear the successive dash of the breakers with foam and fury around the throne of God, which stands out in eternal immoveability (2). We irresistibly contrast this with Canute's throne, which had to be drawn back and back from before the incoming tide.

4. *The Lord is mightier than . . . many waters.*—"As thunder is louder than the loudest noise of the sea, so is Jehovah infinitely more mighty and glorious than the sea, and the worldpower which it symbolizes." The miracle of Jesus in quieting the storm has symbolic and far-reaching meaning. What! do you fear one man, when this God is yours? (Isa. 51:12).

5. *Thy testimonies* (Psa. 19:7; 25. 10).—The sureness of God's testimonies is emphasized here, because the Psalmist would remind us that among their other contents is the sure promise that our foes shall not prevail. Over twenty times God's testimonies are named in Psa. 119.

Holiness is here used in the sense of separation from every evil thing, a condition which God's honor requires Him to maintain. And is there not a pledge implied that He will maintain intact the separateness of the temple of the heart? (I Cor. 6: 19, 20).

Psalm 94 "THY MERCY HELD ME UP"

This Psalm belongs to the same era as the foregoing one. The mention made of the *throne of iniquity* (20) seems to indicate that the Chaldean empire had already arisen, and taken up a threatening attitude against the people of God. Still there is no mention made as yet of the destruction of the temple, or of the leading into captivity; and therefore, perhaps, the land had not been overrun by the invader.

Luther says: "This Psalm is a prayer of all the pious children of God, and of spiritual people, against their persecutors; so that it may be used by all such from the beginning to the end of the world."

1. *God, to whom vengeance belongeth.*—God's vengeance includes the vindication of the eternal law of righteousness, and also of his downtrodden people. We seem to hear already the cry of the martyred saints, "How long, O Lord, holy and true!" (Rev. 6:10). This confident anticipation of God's ultimate decision on the behalf of his down-trodden people is very characteristic of these Psalms.

5. *They afflict thine heritage.*—We are God's heritage, as He is ours. Alas! that after so much culture we return such a poor revenue (Deut. 32:9).

7. *They say, The Lord shalt not see.*—Wicked men are ostrich-like (Psa. 10:11; 59:7).

8-11. *When will ye be wise?*—The Psalmist reasons with those who are both hard of heart and dull of understanding.

12. *Blessed is the man whom Thou chastenest.*— What a schooling is this; and what a Teacher! The discipline is rather severe; but the pupils turn out well, and derive lasting blessedness and rest. Better chastisement than "adversity" (13).

14. *The Lord will not cast off . . . neither forsake.*—God cannot be surprised by anything He discovers in us. He knew all when He began to love us. The tenacity of his love to his chosen people is a strong encouragement to all the seed (Mal. 2:16; John 10:28).

16. *Who will rise up for me?*—This verse is answered by the next two.

19. *My thoughts—Thy comforts.*—Turn from anxious care to the bosom of thy God, till thy soul begins to sing with holy delight.

22, 23. *The Lord is my defence.*—We may very well possess our souls in patience, and not be disturbed by the plottings of our foes: their time is short, their end sure. But oh the pity that they should incur such a fate at the hands of the God of love!

Psalm 95 "LET US SING UNTO THE LORD!"

Few of the Psalms have entered so deeply into the worship of the Church as this. It abounds in bold metaphors and comparisons, calculated to awaken praise as well as heart-searching. The two halves of the Psalm, consisting of five verses each, are united by a middle verse (6), which summons to worship.

1. *The Rock of our salvation.*—God is a Rock, by virtue of his steadfastness and unchangeableness.

2. *Let us come before his presence!*—His presence never casts a shadow, but prompts to joy. Live in the perpetual realization of

that presence, if you would have perennial gladness (Psa. 16:11: *see also* Exod. 33:14, 15).

4, 5. *The deep places of the earth*: *the strength of the hills.*—Depths and heights; sea and land—are full of God. However high we climb or low we descend, in whatever condition we find ourselves, there is always certain evidence of God and a theme for praise.

6. *Oh come, let us worship!*—When the heart is full, it brims over in some outward act of devotion.

7. *We, the people of his pasture.*—*His pasture*, *i.e.*, the flock whom He feeds and tends; his hand, *i.e.*, with which He counts, and guides, and defends. Ah, remember how the Shepherd's hand was pierced, and still bears a scar!

8-10. *Harden not your heart!*—For the day of Meribah and Massah (R.V.) we must turn to Exod. 17:7. From the last clause of verse 7 to the end of the Psalm will be found quoted in Heb. 3:7-11.

11. *My rest* is surely that into which God entered at creation. It has been the chosen object of search for all mankind. But it certainly was not exhausted or fulfilled in the rest of Canaan; for here, though the people had been settled in that land for centuries, God speaks of their missing his rest. Obviously, then, they had not yet entered it; and it remains for all who believe in the true Joshua, Jesus our Lord (Heb. 4:9, 10).

Psalm 96 "THE BEAUTY OF HOLINESS"

This Psalm and the preceding one form a pair. This one is to be also found in I Chron. 16:23-33. It was probably re-edited at the time when the preceding Psalm (95.) was composed. Note the thrice-repeated command, *Sing, sing, sing* (1, 2), which corresponds to the thrice-repeated, *Give, give, give* (7, 8); and with the triple call for joy from heaven, sea, and field (11, 12).

1. *Sing unto the Lord a new song!*—We should always praise God with fresh emotions, if not with different words. The "new song" is ever in front of us (Rev. 5:9, 10).

2. *Show forth*, not only with our lips, but with our lives.

5. *Idols, i.e.*, "things of nought" (R.V., *marg.*). *See* I Cor. 8:4-6.—The *heavens* are constantly quoted as a challenge to our poor conceptions of God (Job 26; Isa. 40).

6. *Honor and majesty* are his inseparable attendants; and wherever He is (for here is his sanctuary) there are strength and beauty. These may also be ours as his gifts (9), but to give them back to Him (7).

7, 8. *Give unto the Lord!* (*compare* Psa. 29:1, 2).—What better offering is there than thyself? (Rom. 12:1).

10. *The Lord reigneth!*—The reign of the Lord in heart or universe must ever be a theme for song. His righteous equity shall yet roll back the curse, and hush the groans of a travailing universe (Rom. 8:14-22). "Tell it out!"

Psalm 97 "LET THE EARTH REJOICE!"

The reign of Christ affects all material things. Alas that men are so slow to acknowledge it (1-6)! the votaries of false gods are bewildered (7); but the people of God are glad, and are encouraged to endure steadfast to the end (8-12).

1. *The Lord reigneth!*—How different is the Psalmist's exultation at God's reign, to the fear which many have when asked to yield Him the supreme empire of their hearts! (Luke 19:14). And yet the strain of Hallelujah is impossible till it can be said in heart and universe, "The Lord God Omnipotent reigneth" (Rev. 19:6).

2. *Clouds and darkness* are often around God still (Deut. 4:11; Psa. 18:11); but we can trust Him, because we know that all He does is based on righteousness and truth (*see* II Sam. 22:12).

4, 5. *The earth trembled: the hills melted.*—*Compare* Hab. 3:6.

7. *Worship Him, all ye gods*—This is quoted in the Epistle to the Hebrews, as an address to *Angels* (Heb. 1:6), a circumstance which is doubtless owing to the quotation being made from the Septuagint. And the fact of this Psalm being there applied to our Lord is a striking evidence of his equality and oneness with

Jehovah; and warrants us in inserting his name in all these Psalms. "The Lord *Jesus* reigneth!"

8-12. *Zion was glad! . . . rejoice, ye righteous!*—The kingdom of Jesus, like the pillar of fire, has a dark side for Egyptians, and a bright one toward the Israel of God.

10. *He preserveth! He deliverth!*—The character, safety, and deliverance of the child of God. Herein the great Apostle rejoiced (II Tim. 4:18).

11. *Light is sown for the upright.*—Coal is *sown light* in the natural world; and so tears, griefs, trials, are the seeds from which the saints shall reap crops of future blessedness. But the harvest day is not yet (Heb. 12:11; Jas. 5:7, 8).

12. *Rejoice! . . . give thanks!*—The holiness of God, which was once against us, is now on our side, and is the theme of our praise.

Psalm 98 A NEW SONG

In this Psalm the whole creation is summoned to be one great orchestra of praise. It seems as if this summons might have been addressed to all living things, as the elders first began to praise the Lamb in the midst of the Throne (Rev. 5:12, 13).

1. *Marvellous things.*—Who can recount them when they include such marvels as redemption, forgiveness, deliverance from the power of sin, the overthrow of Satan, and the glory of God through the mystery of pain and evil? The *right hand* that was nailed to the cross. The *holy arm* that would not ward off a single blow levelled at Himself.

2. *His salvation—His righteousness.*—It is a great salvation, based on the satisfaction of the noblest moral perfections in God's nature. "He is just, and the justifier of him that believeth." In the face of earth and hell, He has openly shown Himself Saviour.

3. *Mercy and truth.*—What a wonderful combination! But it is not the house of Israel only who are permitted to participate in them. Gentiles also at the furthest distance may see and receive.

4. *All the earth.*—The hum of bees, the rustle of woods, the

murmur of rivers, the boom of ocean waves, are constituent voices in the "joyful noise" of "all the earth." Inarticulate to man, but precious to God.

6. *A joyful noise before the King.*—There are some who speak as if the Kingship of the Lord Jesus were a subject for melancholy. They dread nothing more than to be the absolute slaves of such a master. How much more faithful is the conception of the Psalmist —that it should be the theme of song!

9. *He cometh.*—— To those that love Him, his coming is a theme of joy. This refrain is repeated from Psalm 96; as if the pious heart can never tire of so sweet a theme. And well may inanimate nature be glad; for though now, as Goethe said, she is a captive waiting for her redemption, when Jesus comes, her groaning and travail will be ended, and her curse removed.

Psalm 99 "EXALT YE THE LORD!"

This is the last of these precious Psalms which dwell so rapturously on the reign of Jesus. It falls into three strophes, each of which ends with an ejaculation upon the holiness of God (3, 5, 9).

1-3. *The Lord is great in Zion.*—The majesty of God. But great and awful though He be, we fear Him not; for "He sitteth on the cherubim," a phrase which always recalls the blood-besprinkled mercy-seat—God in Christ, reconciling the world. Though the reign of Christ is closely associated with the temporal restoration of Israel, yet in the meanwhile it is set up in the hearts of believers (Luke 12: 32; 17:21; II Cor. 10:5).

4, 5. *Exalt ye the Lord! . . . and worship!*—A demand for homage. The more we abase ourselves before God, the more we exalt Him: and we have good reason to do so, whether we consider the attributes of his character, or the distance between his holiness and our sin.

6-9. *They called: He answered.*—An enforcement from the examples of the past. There never were three such men; and each was a marvellous illustration of the power of prayer and praise. Let us follow in their footsteps, cultivating the meekness of Moses;

the holy nearness of the Aaronic priesthood; and the prayers which were so striking a characteristic of Samuel (I Sam. 7:8-13; 8:6, 21).

8. *Thou forgavest! Thou tookest vengeance!*—Let us beware of sin; it may be forgiven, yet we may have to reap its bitter results. Moses was forgiven, but he did not enter the Promised Land; so was David, but the sword never left his house.

9. *His holy hill! . . . Our God is holy*!—Oh, the holiness of God! Let us not rest until it has been brought into our hearts by the Holy Ghost; so that we may be holy in quality, if not in degree, as God is holy (I Pet. 1:16).

Psalm 100 "WITH THANKSGIVING!"

In the previous Psalm three is a commendation of our Lord Jesus and of the majesty of his kingdom; in this, there is an exhortation, based on that royal conception, for "all the earth" to worship Him. It is full of holy rapture, and has inspired hearts to love and worship through all ages. May our hearts be in tune with the anthem of the universal church, as we peruse these noble and majestic words! But it may be that it has been specially prepared as an anthem for use in that golden coming time, when the kingdoms of this world shall indeed have become the kingdoms of the Son of Man.

1. *All ye lands!*—It is especially on the Lord's day that the devout heart thinks of all the lands of men on whom its blessed light is breaking, and asks that the "joyful noise" of loyal and glad hearts may rise from each. All lands have been included in the purchase of Calvary: let *all* sing! (Rev. 7:9).

2. *Serve the Lord with gladness! . . . with singing!*—God's service is glad—joyous, blessed, perfect freedom. Let us not do his will grudgingly, but gladly.

3. *Know ye that Jehovah is Elohim*: that the Self-existent One is also the Almighty One! The more we know God, the more able shall we be be to praise Him. Notice the themes for praise:—

(1) That He is God; the only living and true God; infinitely perfect: self-existent and self-sufficient; the Father of mercies,

tender and true, loving and strong—Oh, rapture indeed, that such a one is God!

(2) That He is our Creator; because as such He is responsible for us.

(3) That He is our Proprietor. *He hath made us; and we are his* (R.V.).

(4) That we are his people—owning Him, therefore, as our liege Lord and King. "Rejoice greatly, daughter of Zion: thy King cometh!" (Zech. 9:9).

(5) That He is our Shepherd: and it is the Shepherd's part to care—not the sheep's.

4. *Enter into his gates!*—We specially enter his gates, when we mingle with the assemblies of his people. Put on the garment of praise with other Sunday attire!

5. *The Lord is good!*—Yes, good always and only: equally so when He takes as when He gives; when He chides as when He smiles. And what He has been, He will be. He is the "faithful" God (I Cor. 1:9; I Thess. 5:24; II Thess. 3:3; I Pet. 4:19). Praise Him!

Psalm 101 "MERCY AND JUDGMENT"

Again we come on one of David's Psalms. This was not improbably composed at the beginning of his reign, and contains the ideal programme which he proposed to himself; and the principles here laid down are those which not only apply to every Christian community, but which will assuredly distinguish the kingdom of the blessed Lord, for whose advent the Church daily prayeth.

1. *I will sing of mercy and judgment.*—Mercy and judgment marvelously blend in all human lives; and they should be alike commemorated in song. Sing your songs to God!

2. *I will behave myself wisely.*—The art of this is given (Psa. 119:99; *see also* I Sam. 18:14, 15). The reward of such conduct is the coming of God into the soul (Exod. 20:24; John 14:23). But the pious heart yearns for it to make haste and arrive. *Oh, when whilt Thou come unto me? A perfect heart* is the

blameless, consecrated, and wholly yielded heart (I Kings 3:14; Prov. 20:7).

3-8. *I will set no base thing before mine eyes!*—Here is the picture of a pious palace, or private dwelling-house. No slander or pride; upright and trustworthy servants; deceit and lying banished; and strict discipline maintained (1 Tim. 3:4).

We may well ask ourselves whether this is a true picture of the inner realm of the heart, and whether we are strict and merciless in not permitting traitors there. We do not now use the sword of extermination to men; but we should for evil principles and habits, and unholy things.

Psalm 102 "WITHERED LIKE GRASS"

This is the fifth of the penitential Psalms. Some have held that it is one of the later Psalms, asking for deliverance from the captivity; but, from certain special Davidic characteristics, it seems better to refer it to the hand of the royal and sweet Psalmist himself. However, its authorship is of comparatively small consequence; the main thing is to notice the adequateness of the Psalm to those who are afflicted and overwhelmed, and who feel the need of suitable words in which to pour out their hearts to God.

We may arrange the subjects as follows:—A pitiful complaint (1-11); confidence in the Divine Deliverer (12-22); a comparison of the greatness of God with the frailty of nature (23-28).

4. *My heart is smitten.*—A withered heart, from which all joy is gone, as the juice from a sapless bough (*see* verse 11).

5. *My bones cleave to my flesh* (*see* Job. 19:20; Lam. 4:8).

6, 7. *I am like a pelican, . . . an owl, . . . a sparrow.*—All symbols of solitariness.

7. *Alone upon the housetop.*—Loneliness is one of the keenest of human sorrows (Psa. 38:11; John 16:32).

10. *Thou hast lifted me up, and cast me down.*—The devout soul turns from its sorrows to Jehovah. God is ever coming to the soul through human agents and secondary causes. And it deals with Him at first hand.

12. *But Thou, O Lord, sittest as King* (R.V., *marg.*). What a

comfort to turn from our failures and defeats to that eternal Monarchy, which is as independent of us as the stability of the mountains is of the withered leaves that strew their slopes.

13. *Thou shalt arise!*—As much of this complaint was probably occasioned by the depressed state of the Jewish nation, so comfort is occasioned by a clear conviction that the Divine Deliverer is at hand.

14. *Thy servants take pleasure in the stones of Zion.*—When God leads his people to bemoan their low estate, a revival is near at hand (*compare* Neh. 1:3, 4, with 12:43).

15, 16. *So the heathen shall fear the name of the Lord!*—The revival of God's people is indispensable to the awakening of the world. And God's glory is conspicuously manifested in the newly-imparted zeal and life of his servants. Then He indeed appears in glory.

17. *The prayer of the destitute* (Psa. 34:6).

18. *Written for the generation to come* (Matt. 26:13; Rom. 15: 4; I Cor. 10:11).

19, 20. *From heaven did the Lord behold the earth.*—The Lord (*Jah*) stoops low to hear the sighs which might seem too slight to penetrate the dungeon wall. Sigh, imprisoned heart, if thou canst not pray! Sighs fly swift to the ear of God.

25-27. *Of old hast Thou laid the foundation of the earth.*—These magnificent verses are applied directly to our Lord (Heb. 1:8, 10-12). Granite rocks and stars of light shall fulfil their purpose, and be laid aside as worn-out robes when He speaks their concluded mission (Rev. 21:5); but Jehovah-Jesus will ever be unchangeably the same, and able to summon new creations into being with a word.

Psalm 103 THE PSALM OF GRATITUDE

David's name heads this peerless Psalm of praise, which expresses, as none other, the soul of the Church and of the Christian. It has been compared to a still, clear brook of praise.

1. *All that is within me, bless his holy name!*—Let no faculty of the soul be still in God's praise.

2. *Forget not all his benefits.*—Alas! that we forget so often and so many of God's benefits! Memory, awake! and touch thy chords; bring back the blessed past!

3-5. *Who forgiveth! . . . who redeemeth! . . . who satisfieth!*—Notice the "present tenses" in this and the following verses. God's tender dealings run parallel with our lives. He is never weary or exhausted. Enumerate the blessings which He gives, and as the fingers tell the successive beads, praise Him: forgiveness; healing (Exod. 15:26); redemption; crowning; satisfaction (Psa. 36:8; Isa. 58:11); perennial youth. We need not think that the Bible authorizes the belief that the eagle literally renews its youth; but only that the youth, when renewed, is eagle-like in its royal strength (Isa. 40:31).

7. *He made known his ways unto Moses!*—*Ways,* or plans, are only made known to the inner circle of the saints; the ordinary congregation learn only his doings (John 15:15).

8. *The Lord is merciful and gracious,*—A conception of God, which seems strange in its setting of that old Jewish economy, but has been confirmed by all subsequent ages.

9. *He will not always chide.*—He does chide, and we might question his love if He did not. His chiding is occasioned by our sins; and so soon as they are confessed and put away, there is no trace of it left.

10. *He hath not dealt with us after our sins.*—Surely each one can set his seal to this.

11, 12. *As the heaven is high above the earth! . . . As far as is east from west!*—These are the largest measurements which imagination can conceive; but they are all too small for the purpose of the Psalmist, in his desire to describe the impossibility of forgiven sin coming back on the soul.

13, 14. *Like as a father pitieth . . . so the Lord pitieth.*—We do not half enough realize our Father's pity. We chastise ourselves bitterly if we do not understand or reach our ideals. We are ever fearful that He will not give us credit for the motives which underlie our sad and fitful experience. We try to make ourselves more fit for his love. And all the time He is tenderly regarding us, and knows so well how much of our failure accrues from temperament, and disposition, and overstrain (I Kings 19:5).

15-18. *As for man, his days are as grass.*—What a sublime contrast between man's weakness, at his best—and God's eternity of mercy! There is a promise also here for the grandchildren of God's people.—*Remember to do.*

19. *His Kingdom ruleth over all.*—Yes, all men and devils are beneath that power. Satan must even get permission before he can tempt (Job 1:11, 12; Luke 22:31).

20. *Bless the Lord, ye his angels!*—The mighty and obedient angels! Angelic obedience might well stimulate us (Matt. 6:10).

22. *Bless the Lord, all his works!*—One lonely soul on fire with the love of God may set the whole universe ablaze (Acts 2:41; Rev. 5:11).

Psalm 104 "HOW MANIFOLD ARE THY WORKS!"

An anonymous poem; and yet there are many indications of David's touch. Luther has well described it as "a praise of God from the book of Nature." The theme is the greatness of God, as seen in his works. The description follows closely on the description of the several days of creation, as given in Gen. 1., the deviations being accounted for by the special object in the Psalmist's mind, of exalting the greatness of God—not only in the creation, but in the maintenance of his universe.

There is a majestic introductory verse, which is then elaborated —First, the light, the heaven and earth, then the formation of the dry land (2-5); the watering of the earth from His fountains (6-9); the provision for beasts and men (10-24); the wonders of the sea (24-26); God's personal work in nature (27-30); a noble conclusion of praise (31-35).

It is almost impossible in the brief space at disposal to say aught of this marvellous production. Here poetry at its highest, sublimity of conception and diction, and devotional feeling of the most spiritual order blend in one superb and unrivalled poem.

2. *Who covereth thyself with light.*—God has many "garments"

ascribed to Him (Psa. 93:1); but this primeval one is, perhaps, the most beautiful of them all.

4. *Who maketh winds his messengers; his ministers a flaming fire* (R.V.).—The tempest and the flame are his slaves; make friends with their Master.

6-8. *At thy rebuke the waters fled.*—This is the work of the third day—the removal of the water from the earth—and is painted at great length, because the Psalmist sees in it an allegory of the removal of the heathen, who had inundated the Holy Land (Psa. 93). Some have seen in these verses a reference to glacial action, by which so much water is being brought down from the mountains to the valleys.

9. *That they turn not again* (Gen 9:15; Job 38:8-11).

11, 12, 14. *Wild asses, . . . fowls, . . . cattle.*—If God is so careful of birds and beasts, how much more of his children! (Matt. 6:26; 10:31).

15. *Wine, . . . oil, . . . bread.*—The products of the land: the olive; the vine; and corn (Deut. 11:14).

16. *The trees of the Lord; the cedars of Lebanon.*—The earth is *satisfied* (13); the trees are *satisfied* (R.V.); all living things are *satisfied* (28, R.V.).

17, 18. *The birds, . . . the wild goats, . . . the conies.*—He who implants natural instincts, provides for their satisfaction.

20-23. *The beasts of the forest creep: the young lions roar.*—Night and morning in the forest pasture-lands.

24. *How manifold are thy works!* (Psa. 111:2). The fertility of God's inventiveness.

28. *Thou openest thine hand.*—To satisfy creation, God has but to open his hand.

30, 31. *The Lord shall rejoice in his works.*—Where no human foot treads, God's Spirit broods, rejoicing in his works.

34. *My meditation of Him shall be sweet.*—Here, indeed, is food for holy meditation; sweet because of its theme. Let us also rejoice in the Lord!

Psalm 105 THE COVENANT WITH ABRAHAM

This Psalm is supposed to date from the Babylonian captivity, at which time the hearts of God's people would be specially directed to that faithfulness which could not fail (Psa. 89:33), and must keep for them all that it had promised. It was natural then to recapitulate the past as an argument for a similar interposition again on their behalf.

The past wonders of God are quoted as arguments for the future (1-7); a recalling of the covenant (8-12); his care over the early Jewish fathers (13-15); his guidance of Jacob and his family to Egypt (16-23); the deliverance of Israel with great wonders and signs (24-38); the marvels of the wilderness march (39-42); and the introduction of Israel into Canaan (43-45).

2. *Sing unto Him! sing psalms unto Him!*—If you cannot sing, talk.

3. *Glory ye* (lit. *Praise ye!* same word as translated *Boast in*, Psa. 34:2).—In the midst of our deepest trouble we have reason for joy; and even the seeker has plenty to rejoice over, for he is on a road which must lead him ultimately to blessedness.

8. *He hath remembered his covenant.*—A verbal allusion to Deut. 7:9.

9. *Which He made with Abraham.*—When once you can lay hold of a promise, or the provisions of the covenant, you have a leverage with God which enables you to count upon the fulfilment of your petition. God cannot go back from his plighted word.

12. *But a few men; yea, very few.*—And His word is entirely independent of our numbers or power.

15. *Touch not Mine anointed ones* (R.V.; *see* Psa.20:6).—How safe we are! (Gen. 20:6).

17-22. *Joseph, who was sold for a slave.*—A summary of Joseph's career in Egypt.

18. *Laid in iron.*—Is this not equivalent to the entrance of the iron into his soul?

19. *His word came.*—Until the time that the thing which Joseph had spoken was brought under the notice of Pharaoh, when his

"discreet and wise" spirit—the veritable word of the Lord (Gen. 41:38, 39)—approved him to the Egyptian monarch. In compliance with his request, the chief butler made mention of Joseph to Pharaoh, and he was "brought out of the prison house" (Gen. 40:14).

23-27. *Israel also came into Egypt.*—The Egyptian experiences of the children of Israel.

28-36. *Darkness; waters turned into blood; frogs; flies; lice; hail; the smiting of the firstborn.*—A magnificent description of the plagues; with several added, and graphic touches.

39-41. *Israel in the wilderness* (Exod. 12-17).

42. *His holy promise.*—If He did all this because of his covenant, it is impossible that He will ever forget or forsake his own.

43-45. *He brought forth his people with joy.*—All the benefits bestowed on Israel are shadows of spiritual blessings. Redeemed; enriched; restored; satisfied with heavenly bread, and drinking of the spiritual rock; made to sit in heavenly places. What can we desire more? Only let us not rebel against Him.

Psalm 106 "THEY FORGOT GOD!"

The previous Psalm was a history of God's goodness to Israel: and this is a history of their rebellions and provocations. Its main character is the confession of sin. If, as is supposed, it dates from the captivity, it is in harmony with the confessions of Daniel and Nehemiah; and it tends to show that the sharp discipline had done its work, and that God was about to restore his people to the land of their fathers.

After an introduction of inimitable sweetness (1-6), the confession extends to the sins of Egypt (6-12); of the wilderness (13-33); and of Canaan (34-43). But as, in spite of all, the mercy of God had so often interposed, so the believer felt able to call on the Lord to complete the work He had begun, and to gather the nation again from among the heathen (44-48).

1. *Oh, give thanks unto the Lord!*—This is also the commencement of Psa. 107: it likewise forms the opening sentence of Psa.

136; whilst in the latter Psalm, *For his mercy endureth for ever* is the oft-recurring refrain.

4, 5. *Remember me, O Lord!*—A prayer like this is sure of its answer (*see* Neh. 13:14, 22, 31).

7, 8. *Our fathers provoked Him at the Red Sea.*—Our sin cannot shut us out of the love of God. There is ever a *Nevertheless* (Neh. 9:31; Psa. 73:23; 89:33).

12, 13. *They believed . . . they forgot.*—How sad and sudden a contrast!

15. *He sent leanness into their soul.*—Let us ever condition our prayers in the will of God, lest a similar fate overtake us.

16. *They envied Moses and Aaron* (Num. 16:3, 5, 7).

19-29. *They made a calf; they despised; they murmured.*—How sad a catalogue of failures!

23. *Stood in the breach,* as a warrior covers with his body a broken piece of a wall in a besieged city.

28. *They joined themselves unto Baal-peor.*—This was the result of the suggestions of Balaam to Balak (Num. 25:3; Rev. 2:14).

32, 33. *It went ill with Moses.*—How infectious is unbelief, that it spread from the people to their noble leader!

35-39. *Were mingled among the heathen.*—In spite of Joshua's warning (Josh. 23:12, 13; *see also* Judges 2:2; 3:6).

43. *Many times did He deliver them.*—These are the times of the Judges and the Kings! And how many times has He also delivered us from the results of our sins!

44. *Nevertheless He regarded their affliction.*—Another *Nevertheless.* See verse 8.

46. *He made them to be pitied.*—God can put pity into the heart of your most merciless foe.

48. *Blessed be the Lord God of Israel from everlasting to everlasting.*—With this magnificent doxology we close the fourth book of the Psalms; and as we do so, we worship and bow down, and join the hallelujahs of heaven and earth.

Psalm 107 "OH THAT MEN WOULD PRAISE THE LORD!"

This Psalm, according to verse 32, was composed to be sung at a national religious service, in which joy was the keynote. It was also, according to verse 22, connected with the offering of sacrifices and thank-offerings. It is thought that it was composed for the first celebration of the feast of tabernacles, after the return from the exile, when Israel was gathered as one man at Jerusalem, and sacrifices were offered (Ezra 3:1-3). The special references, however, are not very distinct; and so the Psalm is appropriate to the whole Church, and to each individual, after experiencing some marked Divine interposition or deliverance.

The Psalm begins with an exhortation to praise, on account of God's gracious deeds: and in the following verses we are presented with four tableaux: Of the caravan in the wilderness (4-9); of the prisoner (10-16); of the sick (17-22); of the mariner in the storm (23-32). In each of these paragraphs there is a great similarity of order: first the *trouble,* then the *cry for help,* then the gracious *deliverance,* and, lastly, *the exhortation to give thanks.* After this, there is a glad reference to the restored nation (33-43), which, in spite of the hate of its enemies, had been reinstated in its own land, and was already preparing to rebuild the Holy City.

1, 2. *His mercy endureth forever.*—It is not enough to think it: *say* it.

3. *He gathered them out of the lands.*—Evidently in reference to the return from the Captivity (Isa. 43:5, 6; 56:8).

4. *They wandered in the wilderness.*—We are in this world as in a wilderness, having no continuing city; but we are under the care of One who is leading us through the desert to our home, and He will not suffer us to lack any good thing.

8. *Oh that men would praise the Lord for his goodness!*—This prayerful refrain occurs four times (verses 8, 15, 21, 31).

9. *He satisfieth . . . and filleth.*—Blessed hunger, which meets with such a provision! (Matt. 5:6).

10-14. *In darkness and in the shadow of death.*—Words fail to describe the miseries of an Oriental prison: a true type, though, of souls under conviction; or of the pressure of some great heart-sorrow: yet out of these the Lord delivereth (II Thess. 3:2).

17. *Because of their transgression.*—We are foolish to yield to transgression, which so often brings in its train sickness of body. But let us beware of saying that sickness is a sign of special sin (John 9:2, 3).

20. *He sent his word, and healed them.*—His name in all ages has been Jehovah-rophi, "the Lord that healeth thee" (Exod. 15:26). And He heals the diseases of souls as well as of bodies. Oh, put yourselves into the hands of the good Physician of souls!

25-29. *He raiseth the stormy wind.*—We all know what these storms mean: but they are valuable if they bring us to an end of ourselves; for then we are at the beginning of God.

33-38. *He turneth . . . a fruitful land into barrenness.*—Those who trust in earthly comforts, and seem secure, may in a moment be left destitute; whilst those who are in the greatest straits may suddenly become enriched with all manner of good. Do not trust in things, but in God.

43. *Whoso is wise, and will observe these things.*—Let us ask God to give us this true wisdom and spiritual insight; that we may look out for these indications of Divine mercy, and treasure them for our encouragement and comfort, and as sources of praise.

Psalm 108 MY HEART IS FIXED!

This is a Davidic Psalm, and a variation of the sixtieth. It consists of three strophes. The first (1-5) is borrowed, with alterations, from Psa. 57:7-11; the second (6-9) and the third (10-13) from 60:5-12. This Psalm seems to have been intended to express, on the behalf of the people of God in all ages, their firm confidence that He would deliver them, and ultimately give victory over all their enemies.

1. *My heart is fixed.*—The *fixed heart* is the singing heart. *Glory* here stands for mouth, or soul, whose praise pleases God (Psa. 30:12).

2. *I will awake the dawn* (R.V., *marg.*).—There is no time for praise like early morn. Let us ask God to waken us (Isa. 50:4).

6. *That thy beloved may be delivered.*—We are *beloved* in the "Beloved" (Eph. 1:6). *Me* in the A.V. is changed to *us* in R.V. The saint never prays alone; the voice of Jesus and of the universal Church blends with his.

7. God hath spoken.—When God has spoken, promising victory, we may already begin to exult, and divide the spoils of the war.

8. *Gilead . . . Manasseh . . . Ephraim.*—David enumerates the various portions of the land which already owned his sway, and the other portions which he had subjugated. And in Christ the believer learns that all things are his (I Cor. 3: 21). Even his enemies contribute to his possessions and wealth.

10. *Who will lead me into Edom?*—Most of us have an Edom before us, in the form of some difficulty or temptation; but if only we are abiding by faith in God, we shall discover the secret of entering as conquerors, even into the city of rock (Petra, the chief city of Edom, was cut in the rock).

11. *Wilt not Thou, O God?*—An implied answer to the question of ver. 10.

12, 13. *Give us help from trouble.*—"Vanity of vanities" is written on all human aid, and on our resolutions and endeavors: but if only we will follow where God leads the way, we shall go from victory to victory. He will fight for us and tread down our foes; as when a strong man tramples down the forest undergrowth, and the little children have but to follow in his steps.

Psalm 109 "HOLD NOT THY PEACE, O GOD!"

The internal evidence agrees with the inscription as ascribing this Psalm to David; and like others of the same character, it dates probably from the time of the Sauline persecution. It is full of appeals for the Divine vindication of persecuted saints. These old sacred writers had very clear, strong, views of the enormity of wrong-doing, and did not scruple to invoke the Divine justice against those who perpetrated it (*see* Psalm 28:4). There are sentences which exhibit a like spirit in the New Testament (Acts 23:3; I Tim. 1:20; II Tim. 4:4); but on the whole we are taught by the Gospel to speak more leniently of those who oppress us (Matt. 5:44; Luke 23:34; Acts 7:60). We cannot forget the quotation made from this Psalm (8) by the Apostle Peter with reference to the betrayer (Acts 1:20); and thus we are led to question whether these strong imprecations may not be a foreshadowing of that awful fate which must overtake such as knowingly and wilfully sin against God's children and cause.

The arrangement of the Psalm is very simple. It consists of three strophes, each of ten verses; and a final verse which gives the conclusion and sum of the whole.

4. By omitting the three words in italics, we get a beautiful meaning: *But I—prayer;* as if the one response made by the Psalmist was PRAYER; and so much so, that his existence for the time was summed up in the word.

6-15. *Let him be condemned.*—It is held by some that these verses are a quotation of what was desired by his foes; but it is better to consider them not as imprecations but as predictions, the imperative mood being put for the future tense, agreeably to the custom of the Hebrew.

21. *For thy name's sake!*—What an exquisite prayer! Better let God do for you than do for yourself (Psa. 119:124; Jer. 14:7). God's *mercy* is indeed *good.*

22. *I am poor and needy* (so also Psa. 70:5).

26. *Help me, O Lord!*—Another of these sweet ejaculatory petitions, of which we should each carry a quiverful for daily use.

28. *But bless Thou!*—It is well to be persecuted, if with every curse of man we can detect the silver tones of the Divine benediction, saying, "Blessed are ye!" (Matt. 5:11).

31. *He shall stand at the right hand of the poor.*—How brave is the accused if he enters court leaning on the arm of the noblest in the land! How futile is it to condemn when the Judge of all stands beside to justify! (Rom. 8:33).

Psalm 110 "SIT THOU AT MY RIGHT HAND!"

Luther calls this Psalm "the true, high, main Psalm of our beloved Lord, Jesus Christ." Our Lord Himself says that it was written by David in the Holy Ghost; and there is no portion of the Old Testament more frequently quoted in the New (Matt. 22:44; I Cor. 15:25; Heb. 1:3, 13; 5:6, 10; 7:17, 21).

This Psalm was composed when the seat of government and the ark of the covenant where already on Mount Zion. David had already received the grand promise of II Sam. 7; and there rings through the Psalm a grand anticipation of victory over his foes. But do not all these thoughts fade into comparative insignificance as we read into these words conceptions of the glory, perpetuity, and ultimate victory, of the kingdom of our Lord?

In the 1st, 2nd, and 4th verses the Hebrew word JEHOVAH is rendered LORD: where the second mention of the word "LORD" occurs in verse 1, and also in the instance of verse 5, the Hebrew word is ADONAI—Master, Ruler, Lord.

1. *Sit Thou at My right hand!*—This was the welcome of the Ascension Day—the word with which the Father greeted Jesus. And all through the ages He has been engaged in making the foes of Christ the footstool of his feet. This is not accomplished yet, but it is sure.

2. *Out of Zion.*—It is out of Judaism, the seat of which was Zion—from the narrowest nation under heaven—that the Gospel has gone forth, which has a message to the entire race, and is destined to enclose the whole world in its embrace.

3. *Thy people shall be willing.*—A striking picture of the soldiers of Christ. Their spirit, as free-will offerings. Their attire, in the beautiful and glistening robes of holiness. Their numbers, youthful warriors, numerous as the dewdrops besprinkling the morning meadows.

4. *Thou a Priest forever!*—In Jesus the offices of King and Priest blend (Zech. 6:12, 13). This combination of priesthood and kingship is also the spiritual prerogative of all Christ's true disciples (I Peter 2:9; Rev. 1:6; 5:10; 20:6). His priesthood, however, is not after the model of Aaron; but according to that of Melchizedek, a more ancient, universal, and more enduring type, as the Epistle to the Hebrews amply shows (Heb. 7).

5. *Shall strike through kings.*—The triumph of our Lord is guaranteed by the omnipotence of God. But, alas for that *dies*

irae, that day of wrath! Nevertheless, He must bruise the serpent's head (Gen. 3:15).

6. *He shall judge.*—The Gospel of Jesus must be for our blessing or our bane—for salvation or destruction.

7. *He shall drink of the brook in the way.*—As Jonathan in the wood (I Sam. 14:27) took of the honey and was refreshed, so does our Lord drink of the love and devotion of his people, and goes forward without discouragement to the victory which awaits Him. Have you been as a brook from which He has drunk? Is Jesus refreshed by you?

Psalm 111 "THE WORKS OF THE LORD"

This Psalm was probably written after the return from the Captivity. The circumstances of the new colony were poor and depressing. And the aim of the religious leaders of the people was to get them to look up to God, and expect from Him a gracious repetition of the marvelous works of the past. That word, *works,* is the keynote of the Psalm, occurring constantly (verses 2, 3, 4, 6, 7); also the word *ever* (verses 3, 5, 8-10). When tempted to lose heart, because of present difficulty, let us go back on the former deeds of the right hand of the Lord. This Psalm is an alphabetical acrostic.

1. *I will praise the Lord.*—It is not enough to call on others to praise: each of us must do so, as a matter of personal duty.

2. *The works of the Lord are great.*—Let us search them out—the works of the Lord in nature, with telescope or microscope, on Alpine solitude, and by mountain stream, or in the great world of human life. We must seek, if we would find. For it is God's pleasure to hide things.

3. *His work.*—Notice the singular. All the "works" (2) are the WORK, emanating from one source, tending to one result. "One law; one plan; one far-off Divine event."

5. *He will ever be mindful of his covenant.*— Judge not God by his delays; but by his promises. "He waits that He may be gracious."

6. *The heritage of the heathen.*—What a heritage is ours in Christ! (Rom. 8:17).

7. *The works of his hands are verity and judgment.*—They are "Yea and Amen in Christ" (II Cor. 1:20).

9. *He sent redemption unto his people.*—Type of the redemption of Christ (Rev. 5:9).

10. *The fear of the Lord is the beginning of wisdom.*—The fear of God here mentioned is childlike fear, which dreads to offend, and is compatible with perfect love. To have this is to have a wisdom which enters into God's secrets, and reads his meaning, and understands Himself. If you want to have a good understanding of things, and men, and God, you will get it best by being right with God. The standpoint from which we view things is of the utmost importance to our right understanding of them. The margin gives another reading, *a good success.* But note that all depends on obedience. Those that do, know. Act up to all you know; and you will know more (John 7:17). Do God's will, and He will prosper you.

Psalm 112 "HALLELUJAH!"

The HALLELUJAH at the beginning of this Psalm closely relates it to the preceding and following ones. Evidently they were composed about the same time, perhaps by the same author, and belong manifestly to the era of return from the Captivity. Like the preceding Psalm, this also is an alphabetical acrostic.

1. *Blessed is the man that delighteth in His commandments.*—The only way of delighting in God's commandments is to do them (Rev. 22:14).

2. *The generation of the upright shall be blessed.*—We have ample warrant for believing that though godliness is not hereditary, yet the religion of a godly parent has the strongest possible influence on children, and a blessing is passed on to after-generations (Psa. 103:17; Isa. 59:21).

3. *Wealth . . . in his house.*—Although the Christian dispensation is one of spiritual, rather than of temporal, blessing—it is nevertheless true that "Godliness is profitable unto all things,

having promise of the life that now is, and of that which is to come" (I Tim. 4:8).

4. *There ariseth light in the darkness.*—We may not always see the light, but it is behind the cloud, waiting God's signal (Psa. 97:11; Isa. 50:10).

5. *A good man . . . lendeth.*—There is a premonition here of our Lord's words (Matt. 5:42).

7. *He shall not be afraid.*—The heart which is trustfully fixed on God is not afraid: because no tiding can reach it save through the Father's care; and all tidings must be of the Father's appointment. If you are dreading evil tidings, do not look along the road by which the postman comes, but upward and Godward. Trust is expulsive of fear.

9. *He hath given to the poor.*—There is no great difficulty in giving to the poor, when once we have learned our unsearchable riches in Christ. Oh to be purveyors of these to others! (Eph. 3: 2-10).

10. *The wicked shall see, and be grieved.*—The wicked are vexed, partly because they are aware that the righteous have possessions of which they are destitute; and partly because their own schemes melt way before their eyes, as wreaths of smoke.

Psalm 113 "HE RAISETH UP THE POOR"

This and the five following Psalms constitute the Hallel (or Praise-song), sung at the Jewish festivals, particularly at the Passover and Feast of Tabernacles. It is thought to have been the hymn or psalm sung by our Lord and his disciples after the celebration of the Lord's Supper (Matt. 26:30). This Psalm is ruled by the number three; three strophes of three verses each: three times in verse 1 we are exhorted to *praise*.

1. *Praise the name of the Lord!*—God's "name" is his character.

2. *For evermore!*—This verse proceeds on the supposition that our God will forever continue to develop and unfold his glorious nature, so that there will be always some new occasion to adore Him.

3. *From the rising of the sun unto the going down.*—This pre-

diction is yet to be realized (Psa. 72:11; Mal. 1:11; Rev. 15:3, 4). Then the sun's course as it awakens the successive populations of the globe shall be tracked by songs.

5, 6. *Our God . . . who humbleth Himself.*—How humble should we be! Whilst we familiarly speak to God as our Father, we should never forget the immense distance between Him and us. And yet our Lord stooped through this immense distance to become man! (Phil. 2:6-8).

7, 8. *Out of the dust! . . . out of the dunghill!*—These are almost word for word from the prayer of Hannah (I Sam. 2:8). A woman may lead the songs of the Church.

9. *A joyful mother.*—The "barren woman" here may perhaps typify the Jewish Church in her low estate, or even the Gentile Church (Isa. 40:13); but when God wills, and in answer to prayer, her children are multiplied.

Psalm 114 "THE SEA SAW IT, AND FLED!"

The authorship of this Psalm cannot be traced. It clearly belongs to the period of return from the Captivity; and the writer seeks comfort, under much discouragement, in the recollection of the blessed and glorious past.

1. *Israel . . . Jacob.*—The two names of the patriarch occur in the same vesre. Israel must never forget that he was once Jacob; and all Jacobs may yet become Israels, by the grace of God. We all have our Egypts, and our people of strange tongue; but when the lesson of our bondage is learned, our God brings us out.

2. *Judah was his sanctuary.*—The Eternal finds his home in the midst of his people (Deut. 33:12; II Cor. 6:16; Rev. 21:3). Is thy heart his sanctuary and dominion?

3-6. *The sea saw, and fled.*—A poetical description of the passage of the Red Sea, and of the Jordan; also of the giving of the law (Psa. 68:16).

7. *The presence of the God of Jacob.*—How gracious that God should call Himself the God of Jacob! (Isa. 41:14). The Divine presence is always with us (Matt. 28:20), though so often we are

insensible to its majestic glory. And if earth should tremble before Him, much more should we; not with the fear of slaves, but with the godly fear which dares not grieve his Holy Spirit.

8. *Who turned the rock into a standing water.*—Many such miracles doth He still. The most unlikely things yield the streams which quench our thirst and satisfy our souls. Work such miracles, blessed God, on the rocks and flints which glaciers of trouble have brought down into our lives!

Psalm 115 "NOT UNTO US, O LORD!"

Another of the Psalms which date from the Captivity era.

We may divide it thus:—1, Ascription; 2-7, God (*Elohim*), contrasted with heathen Deities; 8, A portrait of idolaters; 9-11, Exhortation; 12-15, Assurance; 16-18, Resolution.

1. *Not unto us, O Lord!*—It would eliminate from success and praise their power to harm us, if we would, from the heart, give utterance to these noble words. God's mercy and truth are indissoluble.

2, 3. *Where is their God?*—Those accustomed to some visible embodiment of God are always amazed at spiritual worship (John 4:24). Pompey, we are told, was very surprised to find nothing in the most Holy Place. God's good pleasure is never arbitrary, but always conditioned by the highest welfare of his creatures. Let us ask Him to work that pleasure out in us that we may please Him! Heb. 13:21 and 11:5).

4-7. *Their idols.*—This sarcastic description recalls the searching passage in Isaiah 44:9-19.

8. *They that make them.*—A very striking thought is given in these words. We resemble our ideals; we become like what we worship. And though we may not be now tempted to prostrate ourselves before the idols of the heathen, yet there are idols which may fascinate us (I Cor. 10:14; Col. 3:5; I John 5:21). We must not trust gold, or success, or any earthly thing; but God in Christ, till we become like Him (II Cor. 3:18).

9-11. *Trust in the Lord!*—A triple appeal for trust, addressed to the congregation, the priests, and perhaps the proselytes (Ruth

2:12). The greatest cannot do without God. The least may appropriate Him. Trust it taking what God gives. "Help" and "shield" together make a very assuring combination: the one for succour in every moment of need: the other for defence.

12, 13. *The Lord . . . will bless!*—Here is a triple answer to the triple appeal. And we are surely at liberty to argue from the past to the future. What God has done, that He will do: trust Him!

15. *Ye are blessed of the Lord!*—Then let him curse who may. We have but to turn back to Abraham's life to see what God's blessing includes (Gen. 12:2, 3; *see also* Num. 6:22-27). And we who believe must be blessed, if the Maker of all things blesses us. The lot of God's children may seem arduous and darksome; but it is a blessed one: and in Him is our peace and rest.

17. *The dead praise not.*—Views of the HEREAFTER were but partial to the Old Testament saints (II Tim. 1:10). We have now an opportunity, which even heaven does not present, of praising God amid the obloquy and hate of men: let his praise be the more hearty and continuous in proportion to their anathemas.

Psalm 116 "I LOVE THE LORD!"

This Psalm formed part of the Paschal Hallel, and contains an underlying reference to the deliverance from Egypt, and also to the deliverance from the captivity in Babylon. The Psalmist passes from the national deliverance to his personal sweet experiences of redeeming mercy, and sings his own song of thankfulness. The name "Jehovah" occurs fifteen times, and "Jah" once.

1, 2. *He hath heard.*—Answered prayer may well incite to renewed love; but let us not love Him less, if He withhold. Perhaps the withholding is a greater proof of love than giving would be (John 11:3-15).

3-6. *The sorrows of death.*—Many who are reading this Psalm may be in a similar position. And excessive grief is some times apt to check prayer. The soul is too sore and hurt even to cry out. Yet it is well worth our while, when we are in such circumstances, to break through all restraints and call out to God. He is very merciful.

7. *Return unto thy rest, O my soul!*—There is no "rest" so warm and safe for the soul, as in the love and care of God. Sometimes, however, like the dove, we seem to get away from it: there is nothing better, at such times, than to return, and we shall be at once pulled in unto Him (Gen. 8:9). Why do we ever leave our rest? Why wander from our home? (Matt. 11:29). The love of God invites us back (Rom.2:4).

8. *Thou hast delivered.*—He hath delivered; He doth deliver; He will yet deliver (II Cor. 1:10).

10. *I believed: therefore have I spoken.*—Quoted by the Apostle Paul (II Cor. 4:13). This is the speech which convinces men, because it has in it the accent of the speaker's conviction. Never say more than you believe.

11. *In my haste.*—It is this hasty speaking which lies at the root of so much misery to ourselves and others. An eminent director of souls once said: "I shall have good hopes of you when you can speak and move slowly." Oh for a holy collectedness of spirit!

13. *The cup of salvation.*—The Scripture often speaks of our lot as a "cup." In this case it brims with blessed help. But it is only because our dear Lord drank a cup brimming with bitter sorrow (John 18:11).

14. *I will pay my vows.*—A good resolve, repeated in verse 18 (Eccles. 5:4, 5).

15. *Precious in the sight of the Lord is the death of his saints.*—Therefore He often raises them from the very borders of the grave. Each saintly death-bed is the scene of minute care on the part of God our Father; since it is there that He puts the finishing touch on a perfected character. Balaam's wish (Num. 23:10) was not granted; for it went forth from feigned lips.

16. *O Lord, truly I am thy servant (thy slave).*—A marvelous avowal! The Psalmist dwells with delight on his slavery (*ebed,* a slave); and through it finds freedom. To be the slave of Jesus is to taste the sweets of liberty. Those who become God's slaves are loosed by Him from all other bonds (John 8:31-36).

17-19. *The sacrifice of thanksgiving.*—"Praise is comely" (Psa. 33:1; 147:1). Shall we withhold from Jehovah that praise which is his due? Thanksgiving should ever be the accompaniment of our prayers (Phil. 4:6). Verses 17 and 18 are almost identical with verses 13 and 14. We ought not to shrink from making mention of God's name (Psa. 66:13-16).

Psalm 117 "ALL YE NATIONS!"

This is the shortest chapter in the Bible, and its center. Perhaps it was intended to be used as a doxology to the preceding and other Psalms. And yet, small as it is, it is full of a world-wide spirit, reaching out to all nations. "It is a dewdrop reflecting the universe." The Apostle quotes it in Rom. 15:11, as foretelling the call of the Gentiles. In this Psalm, as also in Isa. 11:10, and elsewhere, the spirit of Judaism forgets its natural exclusiveness, and reaches out its hands to the world.

1. *Oh, praise the Lord, all ye nations!*—Before we can appropriate these words, we must have learned to exercise the spirit of praise for ourselves. We must have come to see that the Lord Jesus is infinitely deserving of the love and homage of all mankind. And we must have received into our hearts the spirit of his own great love, which yearns over all men. Men will never be truly happy till they adore and praise Him whom we call Master (Phil. 2:10).

2. *His merciful kindness is great.*—The greatness of his love and the permanence of his word. Here are themes indeed for praise. Do we think enough of them? And are we as prepared to praise in dark and sad days as in bright and happy ones—because God is the same, and the same to us, though our lot may not be quite what it was in other and more gladsome moments?

Psalm 118 "CHASTENED SORE!"

This Psalm was sung by the restored exiles, when they laid the foundation of the second Temple (Ezra 3:10, 11). It is believed that our Lord and his disciples sang this Psalm before He went into the garden (Matt. 26:30; Mark 14:26). It was the last

Psalm of the Hallel, 113-118; and is said to have been used after the Paschal meal. It is very touching to read into this Psalm some of those thoughts which must have filled the heart of our blessed Saviour, as with it on his lips, He stood on the margin of the cold river. Verse 26 had been, but a few days before, sung in chorus by the multitudes who attended the triumphant entry into Jerusalem (Matt. 21:9). That same verse will probably be on the nation's lips when Zech. 14 is fulfilled. (*Compare* Isa. 25:9 with Matt. 23:39). Luther says of Psalm 118, "This is my Psalm, the one which I love." "Jehovah" occurs twenty-two times, corresponding with the numbers of letters in the Hebrew alphabet; "Jah" occurs five times.

1. *He* IS *good.* Hold this fast, in spite of all appearances to the contrary, or the maledictions of his foes. And He will not grow weary, or change (Mal. 3:6).

2-4. *His mercy endureth forever.*—The triple call of Psa. 115: 9-11.

5. *I called, . . . the Lord answered.*— Sin-stricken and sorrowful souls can hardly do better than take this prescription. If it has healed one, why should it not avail for others? (*See* Psa. 34:6).

6, 7. *The Lord is on my side.*—If you would have God on your side, you must take care to be on his side. And when once a poor saint and God are on the same side, victory is certain (Rom. 8:33; Heb. 13:6).

8, 9. *It is better to trust in the Lord.*—If our dearest friend were a rich and mighty prince, how secure we should be! Are we less so, when we entrust all our concerns to God? Nay, saith the Psalmist, not worse off, but better. Put your most secret desires and plans, then, into the hands of Jesus.

10-12. *In the name of the Lord.*—We may say this of our spiritual foes, as well as of all who oppose our endeavors for God's cause.

14. *The Lord is my strength and song!*—A fragment from the Song of Moses (Exod. 15:2). (*See also* Psa. 27:1; 62:6)

16. *The right hand of the Lord.*—Our Mediator sits at the right

hand of God, the position of activity and might (Mark 16:19). That right hand must therefore prevail for us.

17, 18. *But.*—There is always a "but" of merciful reservation in God's dealings with us (Isa. 38:17).

19, 20. *The gates of righteousness.*—The Lord hath many gates, through which the righteous pass, into the inner chambers of his presence (Rev. 21:12, 25).

22. *The head-stone of the corner.*—This verse is supposed to have been suggested by the difficulty experienced by the Temple builders in fitting a certain stone into its place, though it afterwards occupied a very important position in the completed structure. The verse is frequently quoted, and applied to the Lord Jesus (Matt. 21:42; Acts 4:11; and I Pet. 2:4, 7).

27. *God . . . hath showed us light.*—New light demands more devoted service.

Psalm 119 "THY LAW DO I LOVE"

This long and noble Psalm is devoted to the praise of the Word of God, which it mentions in nearly every verse, under one title or another. Ezra probably composed it in order to lead the people better to appreciate and prize the Holy Scriptures. The Psalm is a rich aid to meditation, if read thoughfully and prayerfully, and will be loved in proportion as it is used. Chrysostom, Ambros, Augustine, and Luther have left on record very high tributes to its worth.

It is an *alphabetical acrostic;* and certainly the most remarkable of all the acrostic Psalms in the Scriptures. To make the Psalm easier to commit to memory, its contents are broken into twenty-two short divisions or sections, all the verses in each section beginning with the same letter of the Hebrew alphabet.

It is a pleasant exercise to take up the keywords of this Psalm, which occur throughout its texture, and to dwell on them in all the varying lights flashed thereon by the context in each several case. Take, for instance, that word *Quicken* (*verses* 25, 37, 40, 88, 149, 156, 159).

The following division, founded on that of Pastor C. A. Davis, is proposed.

1-8. The undefiled, and their blessedness.
9-16. The sanctifying influence of the Word.
17-24. The longings of the holy soul.
25-32. A cry for quickening.
33-40. Faithfulness, the result of the Divine inworking.
41-48. Mercies, and their effect.
49-56. Hope in affliction.
57-64. God our portion.
65-72. A review of the Divine dealings.
73-80. The creature's appeal to its Creator.
81-88. Hope in depression.
89-96. The inimitable Word of God.
97-104. The benefits of pious musing.
105-112. Light for a dark landing.
113-120. Human thoughts contrasted with God's Law.
121-128. The plea of the oppressed.
129-136. Thirst for the living God.
137-144. God's righteousness.
145-152. The paragraph of the "Cry."
153-160. An appeal for consideration.
161-168. The believer's eulogy on God's Word.
169-176. A closing appeal.

And it is touching to notice the closing minor cadence, for the loftiest flights of holy rapture must ever come back to a lowly confession of sin and unworthiness (I Peter 2:25).

Psalm 120 "IN MY DISTRESS."

This and the following fourteen Psalms are called "Songs of Degrees," or of "Goings Up." They were, perhaps, composed for singing as the Ark was being borne to its restingplace. In any case, they became the pilgrim songs of the people, who sang them as they went up from all parts of the country to the annual Feasts. May our souls mount up on these songs as on wings! This Psalm, like so many of David's, seems to refer to Doeg, or a man of his sort, whose lies had brought untold mischief to the singer (I Sam. 22:9).

1. *I cried; . . . and He heard.*—Let those that are in destress lay this testimony to heart. One personal experience is worth tons of exhortation. If you cannot pray, cry.

2. *Deliver . . . from lying lips!*—Slander is a vile sin; though even Christian people are not as watchful against it as they should be (James 3).

3. *Thou false tongue!*—The strongest treatment is not too much to be meted out to those who forge or circulate untrue statements, or statements the truth of which they have not verified.

4. *Sharp arrows . . . with coals of juniper.*—A figurative intimation of the punishment in reserve for slanderers. As sure as the poisoned arrow shot by an expert takes its victim, revenge shall overtake such an offender against God and man.

5. *Woe is me!*—By a proverbial allusion, an outcast life is described. Denied the joys of home and friendship, and participation in the ordinances of God's house, the believer is very like a wanderer among barbarians.

6, 7. *I am for peace . . . they are for war!*—Having opened with a statement of the gracious treatment he received at the hands of the Lord, the Psalmist closes with a contrasted reference to man's ill-treatment of him. He was for peace; but his enemy desired war. In like manner, the Christian is frequently made painfully aware of the "contradiction of sinners." (Heb. 12:3).

Psalm 121 "THE LORD IS THY KEEPER"

Another of the Pilgrim Psalms, prepared for the annual festival journeys. This seems to have been specially designed to be sung in view of the mountains about Jerusalem, and is probably an evening song for the pilgrim-band. The keynote of the Psalm is the word *keep,* which occurs six times in one form or another (*see* R.V.).

1. *I will lift up mine eyes!*—We must not be contented with merely looking at the hills—but must look above and beyond them. The loftiest and mightiest sources of help are too low for us.

Nothing short of God will avail for us.

2. *My help cometh from the Lord!*—The term applied to the Lord, as Creator of heaven and earth, indicates his inexhaustible abundance of help. "Despair is madness in any one who has such a God to help him."

3. *He will not suffer thy foot to be moved.*—The sliding of the foot is a very natural type of misfortune, especially in so mountainous a land as Canaan, where it is in the highest degree dangerous to lose one's foothold (*see also* Gen. 28:15; Psa. 26:1; 37:31).

4. *He . . . shall neither slumber nor sleep.*—This is said of Israel's foes (Isa. 5:27); but it is more true of Israel's God. When the pilot comes on board, the captain may turn in to sleep.

5. *The Lord is thy shade upon thy right hand.*—"Shade" is a metaphor for protection from the scorching heat, like Jonah's gourd. God is a Sun (Psa. 84:11); but He is a shadow from the heat (Psa. 91:1; Isa. 25:4).

6. *The sun shall not smite . . . nor the moon.*—Heat and cold stand for the extremes of condition to which we are all exposed. Sometimes everything is warm and bright around us; at other times we are lonely and depressed: but in all circumstances God is sufficient (Phil. 4:12).

7. *The Lord shall preserve! . . . He shall preserve!*—These repeated assurances are to calm and quiet our unbelief, which needs to be told again and again that God will watch over his own. Nothing that happens to us can be evil. Whatever God lets pass through the meshes of his protection must be for our good.

8. *Thy going out and thy coming in!*—The *going out* is for work and service; the *coming in* may be for rest and refreshment. The Good Shepherd keeps his flock through all (John 10:9).

Psalm 122 "PEACE BE WITHIN THY WALLS!"

If the former Psalm was sung of the pilgrimband, when retiring to rest on the last evening, when Jerusalem was already in sight—*this* would be sung one station further on, when the pilgrims had reached the gates of Jerusalem, and halted for the purpose of arranging themselves for solemn procession to the temple.

It is ascribed to David; and internal evidence confirms the inscription. The city was newly built and beautified, and was the seat of David's government. The house of the Lord, referred to in verses 1 and 9, is clearly the early sanctuary, which was known by this name (Jud. 18:31; 19:18).

1. *Let us go into the house of the Lord!*—There is an illustration of this in Isa. 2:3. It was much to have reached Jerusalem, but much more to have a desire to visit the Lord's house; for that was not merely a material edifice—it was also the place where God met pious souls. Oh for this desire after God!

2. *Our feet are standing* (R.V.).—What a difference a step may make! All the difference between outside and inside—between a stranger and foreigner or a child at home.

3. *Jerusalem . . . a compact city* (compare II Sam. 5:9).—This is an expression of wonder that the stately city had arisen so quickly under the genius of David. What shall we not say, one day, of the new Jerusalem, when she descends from God in his glory! (Rev. 21:2).

4. *Whither the tribes go up.*—From the external splendor of Jerusalem the Psalmist passes on to praise her internal glory, in that she was the religious center and metropolis of the nation. The law to that effect had been laid down in the opening of the national history (Exod. 23:17, Deut. 16:16).

6. *Pray for the peace of Jerusalem.*—In the Hebrew there is a graceful alliteration in this verse:—

> Peace in the City of Peace:
> May those be at peace who love her!

as though David would make the beloved name as dear to his people as it was to himself. Prosperity still attends those who love the name and cause of God. In such souls there are already present the elements of prosperity and blessedness.

7. *Peace . . . and prosperity!*—Let us never forget to pray for the good estate of the Church Universal; not in public only, but

also in our private devotions. Such prayers must be dear to her Bridegroom, Christ.

8. *For my brethren and companions' sakes.*—All who are members of that Church are our brethren and friends.

9. *I will seek thy good.*—Let all strive to promote the cause of God by word and life, by exertions and prayers.

Psalm 123 "UNTO THEE LIFT I MINE EYES"

This Psalm must by internal evidence be carried, as to its authorship, to a much later date than the preceding one. It was probably composed after the return from captivity, when Israel was suffering so much from the Samaritans and others (Ezra 4 and Neh. 2:19). Calvin shows the application of the Psalm to the Church of all ages when he says: "The Holy Ghost, by a clear voice, incites us to come to God, as often as—not one and another member only, but—the whole Church is unjustly and haughtily oppressed by the passions of her enemies."

1. *Unto Thee lift I up mine eyes!*—Our Lord looked upward when He prayed (John 17:1); and He has taught us to look up to our Father in heaven. It is his throne (Matt. 5:34). Sometimes we cannot articulate words and sentences; but we can put a prayer into a look.

2. *Our eyes look unto the Lord our God* (R.V.).—It has been truly said that the servant looks to the master's hand: (1) for direction; (2) for the supply of his needs; (3) for protection; (4) for correction; (5) for reward. A very slight gesture is enough to indicate the master's will. Oh to be so incessantly occupied with the Lord Jesus as to need but a sign! There is perhaps also here the thought of the eagerness with which the eyes of a slave watch for the master's signal that a fault has been expiated by sufficient chastisement. There is a striking parallel in the history of Hagar (Gen. 16:6-9).

3. *We are exceedingly filled with contempt.*— Contempt is hard to bear; but we are taught to expect it, as the followers of Him who passed through storms of contumely, but who despised the shame (Heb. 12:2-4). Fix your hearts on the joy set before you,

and "rejoice, inasmuch as ye are partakers of Christ's sufferings; that when his glory shall be revealed, ye may be glad also with exceeding joy" (I Pet. 4:13).

Psalm 124 "THE LORD ON OUR SIDE"

One of David's Psalms, perhaps written during the Aramaic-Edomitic war (II Sam. 8:3-13: *compare* Psalms 44; 60.) Luther says, "We may well sing this Psalm, not only against our enemies who openly hate and persecute us, but also against spiritual wickedness."

1. *If it had not been the Lord who was on our side!*—What an *If* is this! One shudders to think what and where we might have been, without the delivering, preserving hand of our God. If we are on the Lord's side, and walking uprightly, we need never doubt as to whether He is on our side. That we may rest assured about.

2. *The Lord on our side: . . . men against us.*—Weigh these two in the balances, *God* and *men;* and how unworthy do our fears appear! (Psa. 56:11).

3. *They had swallowed us up quick.*—Probably an allusion to the destruction of the company of Korah (Num. 16:32, 33). The word *quick* is old English for "alive."

4, 5. *The waters; the stream; the proud waters.*—Yet, as a matter of fact, the proud waters never have gone over us. They have threatened us again and again; but there has always been a "*Hitherto shalt thou come, but no further*" (Job 38:11). God makes of soft sand a strong bar to the sea. His voice on high is greater than the voices of the waves (Job 38:8; Psa. 93:3, 4). Trust Him! As it has been, so shall it be.

6. *Blessed be the Lord!*—These outbursts of praise are so characteristic of the sweet Psalmist (Psa. 28:6; 31:21).

7. *Our soul is escaped as a bird out of the snare.*—We have often marvelled at the way in which the Evil One ensnares us. Quite unexpectedly he begins to weave the meshes of some net around the soul, and seems about to hold it his captive. And then, all suddenly, the strong and deft hand of our Heavenly

Friend interposes, as we sometimes interpose on behalf of a struggling insect in a spider's web. The snare falls into a tangled heap, and the soul is free.

8. *Our help is in the name of the Lord.*—All the help of Omnipotence is pledged on the side of the weakest of the saints. Lean back upon it, and be strong!

Psalm 125 "AS MOUNT ZION!"

"The Church first sang this Psalm under the oppression of heathen rule (3); but in her own land; from the natural features of which the figures of her security in the Divine protection are taken. Struggling with manifold troubles, which might have led her to doubt as to the protecting favor of God, she here rises above these in faith." Whilst many of her members were true, others had departed from the living God (4, 5). "These circumstances are exactly those which existed after the deliverance from captivity; at the time when the building of the temple was interrupted" (*compare* Psa. 120; 126.).—*Hengstenberg.*

1. *They that trust in the Lord.*—Trust so links us and our cause to God, that we acquire something of his stability; as the limpet, sticking fast to the rock, partakes of the nature of the rock.

2. *As the mountains round about Jerusalem.*—Robinson says: "The sacred city lies upon the broad and high mountain range, shut in by two deep valleys. All the surrounding hills are higher: in the east, the Mount of Olives; on the south, the Hill of Evil Counsel, which ascends from the Valley of Hinnom." What an exquisite picture this is of the believer—God-encompassed; God-encircled; God-girt! And as the mountains made Jerusalem well-nigh in-accessible and impregnable, so is God round about us, warding off the attacks of our foes. They cannot get at us except through Him. Oh that our eyes might be opened to see the invulnerable walls by which we are surrounded (II Kings 6:17).

3. *The rod of the wicked shall not rest upon the lot of the righteous.*—The wicked do oppress the righteous: but their oppres-

sion shall not be permanent; that the righteous may not be tempted to relinquish their righteousness, and relapse into backsliding.

4. *Do good, O Lord, unto . . . the upright.*—God is to us what we are to Him (Psa. 18:25, 26).

5. *Such as turn aside unto their crooked ways.*—Crooked ways are by-paths or private ways, apart from the highways. The commandments of God are as the public road. To travel along them is to be at peace. To diverge from them is certain misery.

Psalm 126 "THE CAPTIVITY TURNED"

The circumstances in which this Psalm was written are evident upon its face. The exiles were still rejoicing with the new ecstasy of deliverance from captivity, and were extremely anxious as to their future. The first three verses express their joy; the fourth is a prayer for complete deliverance.

1. *When the Lord turned again the captivity of Zion.*—A partial fulfilment of Isa. 52:8. There are times when the soul seems to dwell in a captivity which hinders both its joy and its free devotion. And then suddenly and unexpectedly the captivity is turned. The soul is restored, and is as in times past. It is the Lord's doing, and we are as in a blessed dream (Acts 12:9).

2. *Our mouth was filled with laughter.*—God loves the singing and laughter of his saints. Trust and wait! The memory of your present anguish shall be soon forgotten in tumults of joy (Job 8:21). What a contrast to Psa. 137!

3. *The Lord hath done great things!* (Joel 2:21).

4. *Turn again our captivity.*—Much had been done for the exiles; but a large portion of the nation was still in bondage, and heavy disabilities remained on those who had returned. When God has done much for us, we may venture to ask more. The metaphor of "streams in the south" is derived from the rapidity with which, after the heavy rains, the dry watercourses become flushed with torrent streams. Would that to our hearts and churches might come abundant life, as when the snows melt in the springtime and flush the brooks!

5, 6. *Sow in tears: reap in joy.*—The sowing and reaping are figurative expressions for the commencement of undertakings and their results. Often the farmer who sows in anxiety is agreeably disappointed with the harvest. And this is invariably the case with the children of God. They are often in pain and sorrow; but when these are undergone for righteousness' sake, they must be followed by a harvest of joy, which shall be a hundredfold compensation (Matt. 19:29; Luke 6:21). Let the Christian worker not count as lost the seeds he sows, or the tears in which he steeps them. But let all such rest on that word *doubtless,* which is God's guarantee. Precious tears! precious seed! precious reward! (*compare* Jer. 31:9, 12).

Psalm 127 "EXCEPT THE LORD BUILD"

This Psalm may have been suggested to Solomon by the building of the temple. It teaches us to depend in all our undertakings on the blessing of God. The Divine blessing is the only true source of prosperity; and it should be sought on the threshold of every undertaking.

1. *Except the Lord build the house.*—There is no condemnation implied here against our building and watching, but against our doing anything independently of God; or as if we could permanently succeed apart from Him. We must be fellow-workers with Him (Prov. 10:22).

2. *Bread of sorrows* is that eaten amid hard labor; rising early and sitting late thereat; reminding us of the ancient curse. What a picture this is of the anxiety and care which fall to the lot of so many! On the other hand, the beloved children of God, whilst they do not slack their toils (II Thess. 3:12), are yet relieved of the over-pressure of the nightmare of care. When they have done their best, they leave the results to God, and sleep peacefully; and by night, the blessing or deliverance comes to them, they know not how. There is an alternative reading preferred by some: "He giveth unto his beloved in sleep." That is, that whilst those who know not God as a Father are wearing themselves down with labor and sorrow, blessing comes to the faithful even when they are resting and asleep.

3. *Children are an heritage of the Lord.*—We have here an illustration of how all we have is due to the Lord's tender care. Our family life is his gift (*compare* Gen. 30:2; 33:5).

4, 5. *Happy the man that hath his quiver full!*—Figures are multiplied in these verses, which have thus been expounded in rhyme by Tate and Brady:—

As arrows in a giant's hand
 When marching forth to war,
E'en so the sons of sprightly youth
 Their parents' safeguard are.
Happy the man whose quiver's filled
 With these prevailing arms;
He needs not fear to meet his foe
 At law, or war's alarms.

Contending armies of a besieged city would meet at the gate Jud. 16:2; Isa. 22:7). In view of the teaching of verse 3, it thus appears that the comfort and support which dutiful children render to parents is of the Lord's appointment.

Psalm 128 ON FEARING THE LORD

This Psalm has no authorship or date assigned to it. It is anonymous, as are so many of the sweetest hymns of the Church. But it needs no introduction; and it goes on singing through the world, refreshing weary hearts as the streamlets which run among the hills. The burden is the blessedness of true godliness in the entire range of human life.

1, 4. *Blessed is every one that feareth the Lord.*—How continuously throughout the Old Testament do we find blessedness associated with godliness! (Deut. 7:12-14; 28:1-14; Job 1:10; Psa. 33:12; 112:1-3; 115:13-15). Note the words, *every one,* which hand on the blessing to all, whether Jews or Gentiles, who comply with these conditions. The fear of the Lord is born of love, which dares not grieve. It is the inner temper of the devout soul, which always reveals itself in the consistent and obedient walk. We walk in his ways when we walk in the Spirit (Gal. 5:16, 25).

2. *Shall eat the labour of thine hands.*—A gracious promise! Lev. 26:16, 17 and Deut. 28:31-33 present the dark reverse which is the portion of the ungodly. *It shall be well with thee.*—How

often do we meet with this pledge, either direct or implied, in the Book of Deuteronomy (4:40; 5:16; 6:3, 18; 12:25, 28; 19:13; 22:7); and it is once repeated in the New Testament (Eph. 6:3). Faith can grasp this promise, even when outward appearances seem adverse to its fulfilment (II Kings 4:26). *It shall be well* amid calamity and sorrow, in the deepest, and best, and most permanent sense. Isa. 65:18-25 is the "latter-day" fulfilment of this promise.

3. *In the innermost parts of thine house* (R.V.).—Reminding us of the beautiful courtyard or quadrangle of an Oriental house, in which the fountain plays, and around which the vine trails gracefully. *Thy children like olive plants.*—The petition of Psa. 144:12 is for such a blessing as this. And it has its response. "I am like a green olive tree" (Psa. 52:8; *see also* Jer. 11:16; Hos. 14:6). Jesus grew up as a "tender plant" (Isa. 53:2).

5. *The Lord shall bless thee out of Zion!*—Jerusalem, as the center of religious worship, where the temple was, stood as the focus for the religious life and thought of the nation (Psa. 20:2). And its prosperity was intimately associated with that of the people (Psa. 122:2-6). The spiritual and temporal act and interact.

6. *Thy children's children.*—The promise of Psa. 103:17 accords with this verse (*see also* Prov.13:22). Note the word to restored Israel in Ezek. 37:25; in those days aged men and women shall look with complacency on the boys and girls of a third or fourth generation playing in the streets (Zech. 8:4, 5). Happy are those who, even now, can put their finger on the promise in Isa. 59:21, and claim it as their own!

Psalm 129 "THEY AFFLICTED ME"

Another of the nameless pilgrim-songs. The singer looks back on the many and severe oppressions from which Israel had suffered, but from which the Lord had delivered his people (1-4); and therefore faith concludes that, however proudly the enemy may bear himself, God will certainly visit him with utter ruin (5-8).

1. *Many a time have they afflicted me.*—The youth of Israel was spent in Egypt (Hos. 2:15; 11:1; Jer. 2:6). As we look

back to our youth, once so full of promise, how many are the afflictions through which some of us have passed! We little expected them; we thought that we must escape: but we have had our full measure.

2. *Many a time; . . . yet they have not prevailed.*—But how sweet to remember that every affliction has had its deliverance! There has always been a "yet" (Isa. 44:1; 49:15; Jer. 3:1). We will not therefore dwell on the afflictions, but on the revelation which each has given of the strong and tender care of God. Each has been a dark lantern—in which, when opened, we discovered that his light was burning.

3. *The ploughers ploughed uopn my back.*—As the plough tears up the earth, so does the scourge tear up the back. How true was this of Him in whom the ideal Israel was fitly personified—our blessed Lord! Isa. 1:6; Matt. 27:26).

4. *The Lord is righteous.*—Twelve times throughout the Bible this truth is declared in the same words; besides being continually stated in other forms. It is comforting to know that our God is "righteous in all his ways" (Psa. 11:7; 145:17; *see also* John 17:25). Some think that the Psalmist refers to the plough-cords. The enemies would continue their ploughing; but God suddenly cuts the cords, and looses the cattle, and the plough stands still.

5. *Let them be confounded!*—The imperatives here may be read as predictions: "They shall be."

6. *As the grass upon the housetops.*—The metophor of "grass" is borrowed from Isa. 37:27. There is but little soil on the flat roofs of oriental houses; and grass, which may have taken root there, having no depth of earth, is soon scorched. All the greatness of the world's empires is as grass (Isa. 40:6, 7).

8. *The blessing of the Lord be upon you!*—We have here the customary salutation with which passers-by greeted the reapers. But such a benediction would never be spoken over the withered grass of the house-tops: so the wicked shall pass away with no silvery note of love or blessing sounding over their decease.

Psalm 130 "OUT OF THE DEPTHS"

A choice Psalm! There are times in our experience when nothing suits us as these words. When like Jonah we are cast unto the deep, and all God's billows and waves are passing over us; when like Peter we lose our foothold, and begin to sink—then, indeed, we may cry: "De profundis clamavi." The name of "Lord" (either as "Jehovah," "Jah," or "Adonai") occurs as many times as there are verses. The soul, when in trouble, loves to repeat to itself again and again that precious name in which all help and comfort are enshrined.

1. *Out of the depths have I cried.*—Great soul-trouble and sorrow are often compared to deep and tumultuous waters (Psa. 42:7; 88:7). There are times when no imagery so well sets forth our experiences as this: "All thy waves and thy billows are gone over me." But there is no depth so profound that the soul cannot cry therefrom. If you cannot pray, *cry.*

2. *Lord, hear my voice!*—Can a mother so forget her child as not to hear its moan in pain? She may; but God cannot so forget his own (Isa. 49:15).

3. *O Lord, who shall stand?*—If God should simply notice our sins, and not our tears or faith— or, above all, the atonement of Calvary—we should be without hope.

4. *There is forgiveness with Thee.*—Forgiveness does not lead to lax living, but to a godly fear. The forgiven soul dreads to grieve the Forgiver. Mercy is antiseptic to depravity.

5, 6. *I wait for the Lord.*—We are too apt to wait for circumstances, people, things; and to meet with disappointment, because they are apart from Himself. But those who *wait for the Lord* cannot be ashamed. There may be no Theophany; but, as they wait, a new strength and comfort steal into their hearts. Oh to have the eagerness of the watcher for the dawn, as we wait for God! And should not we all cherish this expectancy for the breaking of that eternal morning, when the day shall dawn on which night never falls?

7. *With the Lord . . . plenteous redemption.*—In God there is something more than forgiveness—there is deliverance. He does not

remember ours sins; or He redeems us from their tyranny and consequences. He does this *plenteously*, "with good measure, pressed down, and running over"; overtopping with a deluge of goodness the loftiest Himalayas of our sins.

8. *He shall redeem Israel.*—HE SHALL! It is certain as his existence, as inevitable as his own glorious nature. If He has made, He can and will redeem.

Psalm 131 "AS A WEANED CHILD"

This Psalm is ascribed to David; and it bears in its small compass distinct traces of its origin. But it was evidently constructed before the dark clouds which overcast the close of his reign had gathered. It must have been composed during that "morning without clouds," in which he ascended the throne of a united people. It is a cry for the child-heart; and it becomes us to offer it "in all times of our wealth," when pride and self-will lie in wait against us (*see* II Chron. 32:25).

1. *My heart is not haughty.*—The home and seat of pride are in the heart; but how often it betrays itself in the eyes! (Psa. 18:27; Prov. 6:17, R.V.). *Exercise* may be rendered, *to walk to and fro.* Though David had a promise of universal dominion, yet he took no step to secure it for himself. He resisted every temptation to snatch for himself that which was nevertheless divinely assured. There are many things which are great and high, both in revelation and in daily providence: we are not forbidden to use our reason; but after our best attempts, we must feel that God's thoughts and ways are higher than ours. He could not be God, were it not so. Our true attitude then is one of childlike, loving trust, waiting to be taught and led. And to such a spirit, God's Spirit of revelation will draw near, making clear mysteries which had baffled reason, and left human genius faint and weary in its quest (Isa. 40:30, 31; Matt. 11:25).

2. *My soul is even as a weaned child.*—The weaned child is no longer filled with tumultuous passion and frenzy for its mother's breast: it is content to do without its wonted sustenance, because is has been led to another source of supply. So, when God turns

us from some long-cherished comfort, let us be sure that it is not to starve us, but to give us something more suited to the maturing conditions of our life. And let us not be cross and impatient, but rather let us quiet ourselves; and, if that seem impossible, beseech that his Spirit may instil his quiet (I Pet. 3:4).

3. *O Israel, hope in the Lord!* (R.V.).—The cure for inquietude is to be found in a hope which begins as a struggling ray, but expands into the "for ever" of eternity.

Psalm 132 LORD, REMEMBER DAVID!

This Psalm is evidenly intended as a dedication song, composed for the completed temple. The earlier verses tell of David's purpose (1-7); then follows an earnest prayer (8-10); and at the conclusion we have the Divine response (11-18).

1. *Lord, remember David.*—When any design approaches completion, we should not forget those who were concerned in its first conception, or gathered the materials. God never forgets them; and we should not (I Cor. 3:8). The names of the Apostles are not omitted from the stones (Rev. 21:14).

2. *How he sware unto the Lord.*—David's anxiety is recorded in II Sam. 7:1, 2.

3. *Surely I will not come into my house.*—We ought always to put the interests of God's house before our own. That was a grand character that Naomi gave of Boaz (Ruth 3:18).

5. *A Tabernacle for the Mighty One of Jacob* (R.V.)—How wonderful that God is known as the Mighty One of Jacob! But surely no man stood in greater need of a mighty God than Jacob.

6. *Ephratah* perhaps stands for Ephraim, and refers to the residence of the Ark in Shiloh. *The fields of the wood* is Kirjath-jearim, where in darkness and solitude the Ark was deposited after its return from the land of the Philistines (I Sam. 7:1; II Sam. 6:3, 4).

8, 9. *Arise, O Lord, into thy rest!*—These verses are taken almost literally from Soloman's dedication prayer (II Chron. 6:41; *see also* Num. 10:35). The Ark was an image and pledge of God's presence with his people. The staves of the Ark were drawn out when it was deposited in the most Holy Place, to indicate that its journeyings were complete (II Chron. 5:9). Oh, weary, tired builders, think of the strength of the true Ark of the Covenant, which is Jesus Christ! In Jesus, ascended and glorified, God rests.

9. *Let thy priests be clothed with righteousness.*—Every believer is a priest, and should wear this robe of righteousness (Rev. 3:4, 5, 18; Ecc. 9:8). Every saint is more than a conqueror, and should shout for joy (Rom. 8:37; Phil. 4:4).

10. *For thy servant David's sake.*—This reminds us of I Kings 8:25. God's anointed king asks that he may be remembered, as the far-off interest of David's prayers and tears.

13-14. *This is My rest.*—These verses are the Divine answer to the petition of verse 8.

16. *Her saints shall shout.*—The answer to verse 9.

17. *I will make the horn of David to bud.*—This is the vindication of the promise quoted in verse 11. God never forgot his pristine promise to David. He speaks of it centuries afterwards (Isa. 55:3). Its partial realization was in the maintenance of a line of kings on the throne of Judah (I Kings 11:36). But its full accomplishment is in our Lord, that lamp of God's grace shining in a dark world (John 8:12; *see also* Ezek. 29:21).

Psalm 133 "AS THE DEW OF HERMON!"

This Psalm celebrates the love of God's people. The word "Behold," with which it opens, indicates, possibly, that some lovely manifestation of such unity was taking place under the Psalmist's eyes: perhaps in connection with a great religious festival. It was probably written by David to celebrate the glad reunion of the nation after its long disunion during the times of the Judges and the opening years of his own reign. This Psalm is a fitting anticipation of our Lord's intercessory prayer (John 17).

1. *How good and how pleasant!*—Brethren of Christ must be brothers of each other (Mark 3:35). It is not enough, however, to be one: we should take all opportunities of manifesting our unity to the world—*dwell together*. Unity does not mean uni-

formity; but oneness of heart, and feeling, and aim (I Cor. 12: 4-6).

2. *Like the precious ointment.*—This oil was specially compounded (Exod. 30:22-25). "Precious," not only because of its intrinsic nature, but more because of its typical character as symbolizing the Holy Spirit (I John 2:20, 27). With that blessed chrism our Lord was anointed at his Baptism (Luke 3:21, 22; 4: 18): and it was copiously shed forth after his Ascension (Acts 2:33). Moreover, the results of that anointing have descended to ourselves, the weakest and furthest, who are but as the skirts of his robes (2). Believer, be sure and avail yourself of the copiousness and wealth of our High Priest's enduement! (John 3:34).

3. *As the dew of Hermon.*—The dew which fell on Mount Hermon is cited as being more lovely and holy than common dew. It is therefore employed as a further metaphor of the anointing oil, which had been referred to. And the Psalmist says that the love which was represented by the oil—which, in turn, was symbolized by the dews of Hermon—fell on Mount Zion as the dew on parched herbage, wherever the Lord's people met there in the exhibition of brotherly love. Love in the Spirit is the dew of this world of men; a symbol and channel of the eternal love and blessing of God.

Psalm 134 "LIFT UP YOUR HANDS!"

This is the last of the pilgrim-psalms. It is supposed to be addressed to the priests of the sanctuary—who were prepared to offer the evening sacrifice—by some pilgrim-bands which had just arrived from their distant journey, and had presented themselves in the temple. We gather from I Chron. 9:33 that the temple was provided with a night-watch of choristers, who kept up the worship of God through the silent hours. And surely God has still such a relay of servants, who come on duty and serve Him through the long dark hours of night. The sufferer from whose eyes sleep has departed; the watcher by the sick bed; the nurse—

all these maintain God's blessed worship, when many of his active workers are recruiting from their toils.

1. *Behold!*—Evidently the matter is pressing, and arises from the immediate circumstances of the moment. How eager are pious souls that God should be loved and adored! Night is no reason for hushing praise. God's song-birds will sing even in curtained cages. It is in the dark that the nightingale fills the woods with torrents of liquid music.

2. *Lift up your hands!*—The lifted hand is the gesture of prayer (Psa. 28:2; 63:4). It is not unimportant to study the appropriate expression of prayer, as well as its matter.

3. *The Lord bless thee out of Zion!* —This is the answer of the priests, as they meet the assembled pilgrims, and return their salutations. We can never send up to God our adoration, but that it comes back to us again; as moisture drawn by sunshine from the earth returns to it again in showers.

Psalm 135 "PRAISE YE THE LORD!"

This is a call for praise, beginning with the priests, who stand in the Lord's house (1-4). God's glory in nature (5-7); in his dealings with Israel (8-14); and in contrast with idols (15-21)—is adduced as a theme for praise. It seems rather like a mosaic, as the description of the singers invoked is taken from the previous Psalm; the account of the exodus from the next Psalm; and the description of idols from Psa. 115.

1. *Praise ye the Lord!*—The first word announces the object of the Psalm—PRAISE.

3. *Sing praises . . . for it is pleasant.*—One rendering of the words, "it is pleasant," is "He is lovely." When the heart is full of the love of Jesus, it seems as if the universe were too small to be an orchestra for his praise.

4. *The Lord hath chosen Jacob.*—God's eternal choice is, indeed, a fit theme for praise! and we who have been thus called into the inner circle, that we might bring others there, may well join in the doxology of the Apostle Paul (Eph. 1:3-6).

5. *I know that the Lord is great.*—The soul has convincing proofs of God's glory, which it treasures.

6. *Whatsoever the Lord pleased.*—To its farthest limits, the whole earth is under his mighty working. He draws the veils of vapor over the hills, and shadows over life.

10-13. *Who smote great nations.*—God's deliverance of his people from their foes—and his gifts—are as much subjects for our praise as for Israel's; because we have all had our Sihon or Og, barring our pathway to blessedness—some unwelcome intruder on our peace.

14. *The Lord will judge . . . He will repent.*—A literal quotation of Deut. 32:36. God is said to "repent," when his people turn to Him. The wind may be blowing strongly in one direction across a plain; but it seems to change, when we, who had been walking against it, turn and go with it.

19, 20. *Bless the Lord!*—In Psa. 115 the word was TRUST; here it is BLESS. But this is the regular graduation of the Christian life. *Trusting* ever leads to *blessing.*

21. *Out of Zion.*—Zion is the place where the believer dwells with God, and may represent the whole Church, or any place, however simple, where two or three meet in his name.

Psalm 136 "HIS MERCY . . . FOREVER"

A magnificent antiphonal Psalm, to be sung by two choirs; or by the temple choir and the people alternately; the response rolling in after every stanza. It seems like an interleaved Bible, and teaches us to interleave all things with the thought of the mercy of God. There are evident traces of its having proceeded from the same hand as the previous Psalm; the aim being to incite the hope and trust of the people of God, by enumerating His glorious acts.

1-3. *The God of gods.*—These verses rest on Deut. 10:17. Is there not a trace of the Trinity in this threefold ascription?

4. *Alone, i.e.,* without human help (Isa. 40:12-17; 63:3).

6. *The earth above the waters.*—The emergence of the earth from

the waters was a favorite thought with the Psalmists 24:2; 33:7; 104:6-9.

7-9. *To Him that made great lights.*—Genesis 1:14-18 set to music.

10-22. *A strong hand, . . . a stretched out arm*—The Exodus and the Wilderness Wanderings recounted in a psalm of thanksgiving.

15. *Overthrew* may be rendered "shook off," as St. Paul did the viper.

19, 20. *Sihon and Og.*—Flies preserved in amber! Our greatest difficulties and opponents will one day only be remembered for the love and mercy which they called into manifestation.

23. *Who remembered us.*—Men forget us in our "low estate"; but that is the time when God seems to remember us most.

25. *Who giveth food.*—The provision made for animals, and birds, and all living things, is a proof of the mercy of God. Will He do less for his children?

26. *His mercy . . . forever.*—What an unspeakable comfort it is to rest on God's mercy, which is unaffected by our failures and sins, and changes not with our fluctuations! Like Himself, his mercy is immutably the same.

Psalm 137 "BY THE RIVERS OF BABYLON!"

One of the most touching of the Psalms. It reminds us of the emotions excited in an army on a distant march by hearing the strains of a home song. It was evidently composed by a returned exile. But it is also clear that the destruction of Babylon herself was imminent (8). We are thus led to the conquest of Babylon by Darius (Dan. 5:31), whereby its entire destruction, as foretold in prophecy, was brought within a measureable range. The Psalm falls into three stropes, each consisting of three verses.

1. *By the rivers of Babylon.*—The streams of Babylon had probably a special fascination for the exiles. First, because they were removed from the busy rush of the city, and thus afforded opportunity for reflection; and secondly, because they were an image and symbol of their floods of tears (Lam. 2:18; 3:48). Daniel loved and sought them (Dan. 8:2; 10:4).

2. *Our harps upon the willows.*—This touching metophor has passed into all languages as an expression of extreme grief. Of what use is the harp when the heart is nigh to breaking?

3. *They required of us a song.*—This demand may have originated from the far-famed power of Hebrew Psalmody. Across the desert the news had come of the sweetness of the temple minstrelsy; or, it may be that their captors were anxious that the Israelites should reconcile themselves to their lot, and feel at home in their banishment. But in any case the treatment by those captors had made compliance with their demand impossible.

4. *How shall we sing . . . in a strange land?*—"The Lord's song" is only possible in the Lord's house, where his presence is manifested and felt. To be separated from Zion was to be separated from God; and to lose God was to lose all. When we have lost the sense of God's presence, having been led captive by our sins, we too are sure to lose our joy, and peace, and blessedness. The land of the stranger and the song of the Lord can never be found together.

5, 6. *If I forget thee, O Jerusalem.*—The imprecation here made is on the hand and tongue; on the one if it should be misemployed in playing, and on the other in singing. Would that we were constantly able to apply these words to our Lord Jesus! Why do we remember all things and people beside, and forget Him? Surely we court failure in every other direction, so long as we do not make Him the crown and head of our chief joy.

7. *The children of Edom.*—Edom took malicious pleasure in the destruction of Jerusalem; and the punishment of Edom is often referred to (Jer. 49:7-22; Lam. 4:21, 22; Ezek. 25:12-14).

8, 9. *O daughter of Babylon!*—Calvin says that the Psalmist acts here as the Divine herald of coming judgment; but there seems a flavor of something more personal and vindictive in these terrible words. We can understand the spirit which breathes through them; but it is rather that of the Old Dispensation than of the New (Matt. 5:43-48).

Psalm 138 "I WILL PRAISE THEE!"

This is the first of a cycle of Davidic Psalms, and is founded on the promise of II Sam. 7. Here, as there, the promised blessing is dwelt upon with gladness. The idols, which could exhibit nothing to compare with it, retreat ashamed (1); the Lord has done more to glorify Himself by it than by all his previous wonders (2); all kings will one day praise the Lord on account of it (4); and it is the beginning of a chain of blessings that can never end (8).

1. *Before the gods may*, however, refer to angels (Psa. 8:5; Heb. 2:7); or to princes (Psa. 82:6; John 10:34-36); or to idols (Psa. 97:7).

2. *Toward thy holy temple.*—This reminds us of Jonah (2:4), and of Daniel (6:10). The temple, as being the seat of religious worship and of sacrifice, is symbolic of that propitiation through which alone sinners may approach God. God's promise, prompted by love, and founded on truth, was a fuller manifestation of God's charatcer than any previous revelation.

3. *Thou answeredst me.*—Our God does not always answer our prayers as we request; but He does for us, as for our Lord in the Garden—He strengthens us (Luke 22:43). Let us not forget that He is "the strength of our heart."

4. *All the kings of the earth.*—It is pleasant to think how many of the great of this world have been included in the ranks of the servants of God; and more shall be (Psa. 68:29; 102:15). And it may be that not a few of them shall be found to have been influenced in their choice by the sweet words of David the king. Each man can best influence the men of his own class.

5. *They shall sing of the ways of the Lord* (R.V.).—So great is the glory of our God, that the noblest of this world may count it an honor to carry his train.

6. To have *respect unto* is to "regard." God eyes with loving regard those who are true to Him; but He is repelled from those whose hearts are proud, so as to look on them only from a distance (II Chron. 16:9).

7. *Thou wilt revive me.*—The revival of the soul is the gracious work of the Holy Spirit. How blessedly and unexpectedly these

revivings steal into our hearts; and so often, when heavy trouble lies on us from without.

8. *The Lord will perfect.*—There are no unfinished pictures on the walls of God's studio; no incomplete statues in his halls of sculpture. When He begins, He pledges Himself to complete. His mercy endures forever; so we cannot tire it or wear it out. But our assurance ought always to take on the language of pleading, that He would not forsake.

Psalm 139 "THOU HAST SEARCHED ME!"

It is rather interesting to notice the position of this sublime ode on the omniscience and omnipresence of God. In earlier Psalms David has again and again reminded us of the love and mercy of God, which "endure forever": and here he bids us take heed that we do not make that love an excuse for sin, because his eyes are as a flame of fire. There is the same combination, though in the reverse order, in Heb. 4:12-16.

Observe: the fact of God's omniscience (1-12); its ground on his creatorship of man (13-18); its consolatory aspect, that as God knows the innocence of his people, so He will not condemn them with the wicked, but lead them in his everlasting way (19-24).

1. *O Lord, Thou hast . . . known me.*—What ineffable comfort there is in the thought that our hearts closed to all else, are open to Him! Because, as He can detect the secret source of our disease, He can cure it; and, as He can read our secret sorrow, He can apply the healing balm. "He knows all; but loves us better than He knows."

2. *Downsitting* is our time of quiet rest; *uprising*, the going forth to work. *Afar off* perhaps means that God anticipates our thoughts and purposes before they are matured in our mind.

3. *Thou winnowest* (*marg.*); as if God were ever applying the fan of his judgment to our active life, and to the thoughts which chase each other across our mind in sleep.

5. *Thou hast beset me.*—The All-knowing is also the All-present. We are God-encompassed; God-environed. *Behind*, that none

may attack in the rear. *Before*, that He may search out the way and met our foes. *Laid thine hand;* as if a child were to put one hand over the hollow of another to keep some frail insect from its pursuer (John 10:28, 29).

6. *Too wonderful!*—We must worship, where we fail to comprehend.

7, 8. *Whither shall I go?*—It used to be said that the entire world was but one vast prison-house for the Roman Emperors, so complete was their power. And what hope can the sinner have of escaping God? (Amos 9:2).

9-12. *The wings of the morning.*—Neither change of hemispheres nor distance, nor darkness, can at all alter the soul's proximity to its ever-present God. What bliss this is to those who know Him as Father and Friend!

13. *Possessed* is "formed" (R.V., *marg.*).—The *reins* are the seat of the desires and feelings. How much transpires in that secret workshop! Nothing can be concealed from our Maker.

15, 16. *Not hid from Thee.*—We may refer these words to the mystical body of Christ, which even now is being secretly prepared and composed of many who are as the lowest dust of the earth. And God's book contains, through his foreknowledge, the names of those who are to be incorporated in that mystical body (Rom. 8:29; Rev. 17:8).

17, 18. *How precious are thy thoughts unto me!*—The Psalmist is so occupied with the thoughts of God, which teem in his mind, that he pursues his meditations sleeping as well as waking. And as he starts from slumber, his first bright waking consciousness is that God is by his side.

19-22. *Am not I grieved?*—When we are startled at these strong expressions of David, we may well ask ourselves whether, in our tender pity for sinners, we may not be losing something of his stern consciousness of the evil of sin, and the guilt of the wicked.

23, 24. *Search me, O God!*—This prayer is a worthy termination of the Psalm. *Lead me* is the one incessant cry of the devout soul. "Lead, kindly Light!" We long to get forward on that way which is everlasting, because founded on the permanent principles of Truth, Righteousness, Light, and Love. The way planned from eternity by the Eternal, and leading to the eternal home.

Psalm 140 "THOU ART MY GOD!"

The tone of this Psalm corresponds with the inscription, and attests its Davidic origin. It perhaps dates from those early troubled days at court, when his steps were taken with difficulty, because of the gins and snares that lined his pathway.

The Psalm consists of five verses as the beginning, and five as the conclusion; and in the middle occurs a strophe of three verses, the heart of the Psalm, distinguished by the fourfold use of the name Jehovah.

1. *Deliver me from the evil man.*—We pray "Deliver us from the evil one" (Matt. 6:13, R.V.).

2. *Gathered together*: as Psa. 56:6; and 59:3.

3. *Adders' poison under their lips.*—Who can describe the mischief caused by a false and slanderous tongue? See also Psa. 58:4; Rom. 3:13, 14.

4. *Keep me, O Lord!*—A good prayer for all times (Psa. 17:8; 25:20).

5. *A snare for me, and cords.*—We have every reason to be afraid of Satan, who adds cunning to his malice; and who is not content with hidden assaults, but weaves insidious toils, which may take months to mature—in order to do us harm; and grieve our Master, Christ, wounding Him through us.

6. *Thou art my God!*—The first portion of the verse corresponds with Psa. 31:14. If He is ours, and we are his we may have confidence that He will "hear the voice of our supplications."

7. *Thou hast covered; Thou dost cover; Thou wilt cover.*—Such is the force of the tense used here (as in Psa. 5:11; 139:13). As we go down into the fight, let us never forget that helmet of salvation provided for us by the Lord Himself (Eph. 6:17; I Thess. 5:8). What a contrast to the "head" of the wicked! (9).

9. *Mischief of their lips.*—Slander is like a man starting an avalanche, which ultimately overwhelms and covers his own dwelling (Psa. 7:15, 16).

10, 11. *Burning coals.*—We have not so learned Christ (Rom. 12: 20); but we must endorse the Psalmist's confidence that evil cannot ultimately prevail in God's world: and that, however great may be the momentary triumph of the wicked, they are destined to utter and disastrous downfall.

12. *The Lord will maintain the cause of the afflicted* (Psa. 9:12; 18:27; Zeph. 3:19).

13. *Shall give thanks.*—Not only hereafter, but here and now, do those who love and serve God walk and live in the manifested light of God's presence (Psa. 16:11; Eph. 5:20).

Psalm 141 "LET MY PRAYER BE AS INCENSE!"

Another of David's Psalms. De Wette is led by the language to class it, with Psa. 10., as one of the oldest.

1. *I cry! . . . Make haste! . . . Give ear!*—The word *Kara*, to call, or to cry, continually occurs in the Scriptures (Psa. 17: 6; 22:2). Psalm 3:4 shows the answer. *Make haste!* (Psa. 38:22; 40:13; 70:1). *Give ear!* (Psa. 17:1; 60:1; 86:6).

2. *Let my prayer be as incense!*—The smoke of the sweet-smelling incense is often used in Scripture as a symbol of the prayer of believers, which is precious to God (Rev. 5:8; 8:3, 4). The offering of incense morning and evening, under the Levitical dispensation, symbolized prayer (Exod. 30:7, 8).

3, 4. *Set a watch before my mouth.*—The Psalmist prays for preservation from the danger of lip sins, heart sins, and life sins. God's sentry is God's peace (Phil. 4:7). How wise to make God the doorkeeper of our mouth! (Prov. 4:24).

4. *Let me not eat of their dainties.*—The child of God does not eat of the "dainties" of the wicked; and yet amid tribulation he seems to sit at a banqueting table, anointed as a guest with oil (Psa. 23:5).

5. *Let the righteous smite me.*—"The righteous" is referred by some commentators to God, who alone, in its full sense, de-

serves the appellation (II Sam. 7:14, 15). But it may also refer to that loving care which one believer may exercise over another, in rebuke and admonition. For, "which shall not break my head," the R.V. more correctly translates, "let not my head refuse it." The last clause should be rendered, as in the R.V., *Even in their wickedness shall my prayer continue.* That prayer rises, like a geyser, in winter's frost as under summer skies.

6. *When their judges.*—When the enemies of the Lord are overthrown, they will be the more prepared to listen to words which they had rejected before, but the intrinsic sweetness of which will then commend them to their hearts.

8. *Mine eyes are unto Thee.*—"Looking off unto Jesus" (Heb. 12:2) is a good motto. And it is marvelous how the feet are kept from snares and pitfalls, when the eyes, instead of being fixed upon the ground, are lifted upwards to the Throne (Psa. 119:110).

9, 10. *That I withal escape.*—Another petition that the Psalmist may be *kept.* Prov. 3:26 gives an encouraging promise—"The Lord shall keep."

Psalm 142 "WITH MY VOICE"

One of David's Cave-Psalms. *Maschil* means Instruction. How much instruction individuals and the Church have gained from the strait dark caves in which, in every age, the saints have been immured! The prison and the persecutor oppress the soul of the sweet singer, who yet towards the close catches sight of a brighter and better time.

1. *I cry with my voice.*—In the R.V. each clause is rendered in the present tense. To use audible words is sometimes a great incentive to prayer, stirring up the spirit to more vehemency and concentration.

2. *I poured out my complaint.*—Of course God knows all before we tell Him; but it is our duty—and a great relief—to unbosom ourselves to Him. We often miss the benefit of prayer, because we deal so much in generals, and do not enough dwell on the particulars of our need.

3. *When my spirit was overwhelmed.*—There are times when, however bravely we would bear ourselves, our spirit faints (R.V. *marg.*). What is here said of the "spirit" (*rooakh*) is oftener predicted of the "soul" (*nephesh*). (Psa. 42:6; 43:5); but the dejection and fainting of the spirit is a more sorrowful condition. Yet how consolatory that God knows our path! His eye is ever fixed on its perplexities. He sees its hidden pitfalls and snares.

4. *Look on my right hand* (R.V.).—It was the Jewish custom for the advocate as well as the accuser to stand on the right hand of the accused (Psa. 110: 5; 16:8; Zech. 3:1). Observe the contrast—*no man knoweth; no man careth*: *Thou* knewest my path (3). Refuge failed me; *Thou* art my refuge (5).

5. *I said, Thou my refuge . . . my portion!*—The loneliness and isolation of the soul from all human love often makes it turn the more urgently to God, who can be loved without satiety, and whose love is unchangeable, unselfish, and eternal. How often does God diminish and break off our portion in this life that we may be driven to seek it again in Himself! (Lam. 3:24).

6. *I am brought very low.*—How well did these words befit the lips of our Lord when He descended into the dust of death for us. He was *brought very low* when he became obedient to the death of the cross. "Stronger than I," but not than Thou! His weakness is stronger than men (Psa. 105:24; Jer. 31:11; Luke 11:22; I Cor. 1:25).

7. *Bring my soul out of prison.*—Is there not an allusion here to the history of Joseph? "Lead me out of distress," as Joseph from prison (*see also* Psa. 102: 10, 13; Isa. 42:7; Acts 12:7-9; 16:39). The compassing of the righteous indicates their sympathy with the Psalmist when they press in to offer their congratulations as garlands and crowns. God's mercy to him would be a source of joy to others, who would bind the story on their brows as a festal crown ("*shall crown themselves,*" R.V., *marg.*).

Psalm 143 HEAR MY PRAYER, O LORD!

The spirit and language of this Psalm are so in unison with the earlier Davidic Psalms as to confirm the genuineness of the superscription. It is the last of the penitential Psalms. The pause divides the Psalm exactly, and it may be viewed as consisting of four stanzas, each of three verses.

1. *In thy faithfulness.*—When we are in Christ, the sterner attributes of God are on our side. A dying woman said, "I rely on the justice of God"; adding, however, when the words excited surprise, "justice, not to me, but to my Substitute in whom I trust" (I John 1:9).

2. *In thy sight shall no man be justified.*—The holiest of men have least confidence in themselves (Job 9:3; Phil. 3:7-9). Bernard of Clairvaux said, "So far from being able to answer for my sins, I cannot answer even for my righteousness." There is a sense in which God will never "enter into judgment" with us, because the great white throne has nought to say to those who are in Christ Jesus. Being justified, who is he that condemneth? (Rom. 5:1; 8:34).

3. *As those that have been long dead.*—The dead are soon forgotten by the living; and David felt that long haunting of the caves and dens of the earth was like a living burial, which was bearing him from the homes and memories of his fellows.

4. *Overwhelmed! . . . Desolate!*—Those who are capable of the gladdest heights of joy are also capable of the saddest depths of depression. David was permitted to touch each, that he might be able to give expression to all kinds of emotion—to every phase of feeling. So was it with our great High Priest, "tempted in all points like as we are." But how unutterable the sorrow of this fainting, desolate heart!

5. *The days of old . . . The work of Thy hands.*—Memory—Meditation—Musing.

6. *I stretch forth my hands.*—Stretch forth your hands; and you will certainly touch God. *My soul thirsteth!* This thirst is blessed (Psa. 42:1, 2; 63:1; Isa. 44:3). To have it is to be satisfied. There is no natural desire which has not its satisfaction; in the woods,

birds do not hunger for food which is not to be had; and so the very existence of this thirst is a proof of the being and sufficiency of Him for whom it yearns, and in whom it is allayed.

7. *Hear me speedily!*—Prayer gets more earnest as it proceeds. *Speedily* does not imply impatience, but vehement yearning. We sometimes think our spirit is going to faint—when there is strength enough left in it to suffer still, and in suffering to attain the strength of steel. But God is very pitiful, and keeps his finger on our pulse while we pass through the operation (Isa. 57:16).

8. *Cause me to hear! . . . cause me to know!*—God's "loving-kindness" speaks continually in the ears of his people: but they may be deaf to it—hence the prayer, "*Cause* me to hear!" (Job 33:16; 36:10; Isa. 50:5). It is well to hear it *in the morning*, before other thoughts enter to engross our attention. Our prayer will be fully answered when the morning of eternity breaks. When you are uncertain about your path, lift your soul into the presence of God, until He saturate it with his light and guidance.

9. *I flee unto Thee!*—Satan outwits himself when he drives us to our God (Psa. 27:5).

10. *Teach me to do thy will.*—It is more important to be taught to *do* than to know. The *Good Spirit's* leadings must be good to follow (Neh. 9:20; Eph. 5:9). The *land of uprightness* is, literally, the level tableland.

11. *For thy Names's sake!*—God's credit and glory are involved in the succor and deliverance of his saints.

12. *I am thy servant.*—God makes Himself responsible for the safety of his servants: therefore to be *his* servant is a better position than to be an Emperor or a Czar.

Psalm 144 "LORD, WHAT IS MAN!"

Dr. Alexander says, "the Davidic origin of this Psalm is as marked as that of any in the Psalter." It is partly compiled of passages taken from other Psalms, as 8:4, and 18:13-15. But the last verses (9-15) are a valuable addition. This Psalm forms a point of transition between the Prayer Psalms and the Songs of

Praise. The cloud of adversity is breaking; the beams of the sun are already struggling through.

1. *The Lord . . . teacheth my hands to war.*—In all spiritual warfare we need to be taught. Our weapons are only mighty through God (II Cor. 10:4). Is there not an illustration of this in II Sam. 5:17-25? (*See also* II Sam. 22:25, 26).

2. *My Goodness, and my Fortress.*—Each of these seven titles for God is a pathway which leads into his very heart. The all-subduing grace of God is indeed a theme for song. The Breaker is ever going before us (Micah 2:13). The Goliaths among men cannot stand before Him, or his weakest servant.

3. *Lord, what is man!*—Man would be insignificant indeed if he were not the favored of Jehovah (*see* Job 7:17; Psa. 8:4; II Sam. 7:18, 19).

4. *As a shadow that passeth.*—The shadows of the clouds darken miles of sea—and anon they are gone. So evanescent, and so impalpable (Psa. 102:11; 109:23; Ecc. 6:12; 8:13).

5. *Bow Thy heavens, O Lord!*—David calls to mind what is recorded (in the past tense) in Psalm 18:9; and here asks God to repeat former deliverances.

9. *I will sing a new song!*—New songs are demanded by new mercies. Let us give God freshly baken loaves for His table (I Sam. 21:6).

10. *Giveth! . . . delivereth!*—*Comp.* Psa. 33:16.

11, 12. *Our sons as plants; our daughters as corner stones.*—In times of war the children are often the first to suffer from privation and hardship. So the king asks for deliverance, that the sons may grow up as vigorous plants, and that the daughters may be as the exquisitely polished corner-stones which connect the walls of a palace, or even as pillars. Nothing is more important than the nurture of a beautiful family life; and for this the deliverances of God on the behalf of its head are all-important. Let the daughters who read these words seek the polishing which comes of God's cuttings. The Prayer-book and other versions substitute the word *temple* for *palace.*

13, 14. *That our garners may be full.*—In this picture of

national prosperity, consequent on devotion to the cause and service of God, we are taught to realize the immense blessing which follows godliness, even in this life (I Tim. 4:8). *Breaking in* refers to the violence of the thief; *going out* to enforced emigration, like that which took Elimelech and his family to Moab (Ruth 1:1, 2). The Hebrew word rendered *oxen* (*aluphim*) may be translated *captains* or *governors.*

15. *Happy the people whose God is the Lord!*—True happiness is only to be found among the people of the Lord, and in the service of the blessed God.

Psalm 145 " I WILL EXTOL THEE!"

This Psalm is a song of thanksgiving and praise on the part of the house of David—and of the Church—after all their tribulations have come to a close. It is an acrostic Psalm, the verses beginning in the Hebrew with the successive letters of the alphabet. Somehow the couplet for the fourteenth letter, *Nun,* has dropped out of the text as it has come down to us. The Septuagint, however, and other ancient versions (with one Hebrew manuscript), supply the omission thus:—"The Lord is faithful in his words, and holy in all his works." The place of this verse is between verses 13 and 14 in our English Bibles.

The word *all* is throughout characteristic of this Praise-song. The Psalm was the *Te Deum* of the Old Testament, and was perhaps the germ of that great Christian hymn. The Jews were accustomed to say that he who could pray this Psalm from the heart three times daily was preparing himself best for the praise of the world to come.

Gilfillan, writing of this and the following Psalms, says:—"They are the Beulah of the Book, where the sun shineth night and day, and the voice of the turtle is heard in the land. Coming at the close after all the mournful, plaintive, penitential, prayerful, varying notes, they unconsciously typify the joy and rest of glory."

1. *I will extol Thee, my God, O King!*—Praise will be the em-

ployment of eternity. There prayer, and faith, and hope, will not be possible; but we shall bless forever.

Our days of praise shall ne'er be past,
While life, and thought, and being last,
And immortality endures.

2. *Every day will I bless Thee!*—Let us not wait for eternity, but begin *to-day;* and let us practise on our harps *every day,* intermitting none, but in dark days as well as in bright! There is always something left to bless God for; at least, there is always *Himself.* Said the poor old woman at her meagre meal, "All this, and Christ!"

3. *His greatness unsearchable.*—The sense is, "His greatness cannot be fathomed." Out of Christ, men can only find out *about* God; but they cannot find HIM out.

4. *One generation . . . to another!*—The generations as they pass transmit, each to the next, the story of God's love and power; and so the record can never die (Psa. 44:1; 78:3).

5. *I will meditate* of the glorious majesty of thine honor (R.V.).

6, 7. *Men shall speak!. . . they shall utter!*—What a tumult of voices! As if the time shall come when the hearts of men shall boil with holy love, and their voices rise in a mighty murmur of sound till they sing.

8. *The Lord is gracious!*—Founded on his own proclamation (Exod. 34:6, 7). We set to our seal that God is true.

9. *The Lord is good!*—Even to the worst; even towards the most insignificant. *Tender mercy* is the blue canopy which arches over all.

10. *All thy works shall praise Thee*!—Creation praises God, but not with intelligence: hence the saints are called upon to interpret her, and to express in language what she would say but cannot.

13. *Thy kingdom is a kingdom of all eternities,* is a sound translation. It will survive the mightiest kingdoms of this world and "stand forever" (Dan. 2:44).

14. *The Lord upholdeth all that fall.*—What a contrast to the preceding majesty! (5-7; Psa. 146:8).

16. *Thou openest thine hand.*—To supply the wants of creation

He has but to *open his hand.* In God the largest appetite is satisfied.

17. *The Lord is righteous.*—In all his dealings with us may we have the faith to dare to say this!

18, 19. *The Lord is nigh unto all them that call.*—What pathos! What exquisite comfort! How nigh He comes! Yet none but the devout soul hears his footfall. *He will fulfil the desire.* He first instils the desire, and then fulfils it.

21. *My mouth shall speak the praise of the Lord.*—Holy praise is contagious; it spreads from lonely hearts to all flesh (Rev. 5:11-13).

Psalm 146 "WHILE I LIVE WILL I PRAISE"

In the Septuagint this Psalm is ascribed to Haggai and Zechariah; and, if they were not the actual authors, these Psalms were probably composed during their times. The term "Hallelujah" (Praise Jah!) is not characteristic of the Psalms which date from the times of David.

2. *While I live will I praise the Lord.*—Our being is to run parallel with God's forever: but we shall never come to an end of his fulness; and so new discoveries will ever incite to new songs.

3. *Put not your trust in princes.*—This was quoted by the Earl of Strafford, on hearing that, in spite of his royal and solemn pledge, Charles I. had given assent to the Bill of Attainder. *The son of man* in this passage cannot refer to the Lord Jesus, for none would dare to apply to Him the succeeding words: "in whom is no help." The Hebrew is distinct: *Confide ye not in a son of man* (*see* Jer. 17:5; John 2:25). The Prayer-book version has: "nor in any child of man."

4. *Thoughts—i.e.,* "purposes" (R.V.*marg.*).—At the moment of death the most definite projects of human life are at an end (Luke 12:16-20).

5. *The God of Jacob.*—Jehovah is thus spoken of twenty-one times in the Old Testament, and six times in the New Testament. If God helped Jacob, He will help the least and meanest of us. The reasons for this happiness appear in the following enumeration.

6. *Who made heaven, and earth, the sea, etc.*—Nearly twenty times the creative work of God is thus referred to in the Bible. Even if we believe not yet He abideth faithful. *Who keepeth truth.* He is true to his promises and covenant-engagements.

7. *Who executeth judgment for the oppressed.*—We need not avenge ourselves; for God will vindicate us (Psa. 103:6; Rom. 12: 19; I Pet. 2:23).

7-9. *The Lord looseth the prisoners.*—These verses are an epitome of the mission of the Comforter (Psa. 68:5, 6; 107:10, 14; Isa. 35:5; 61:3).

8. *The Lord openeth the eyes of the blind.*—What a true portraiture is this of the ministry of Christ through the ages (Luke 4:18; *see also* John 9:1-33). Mark these present tenses! This is his unceasing work. Victor Immanuel—Emancipator!

9. *The Lord preserveth: He relieveth.*—There are traces of this in all the old Hebrew legislation (Deut. 10:18; 14:28, 29; 26: 12, 13; Psa. 68:5). To turn *upside down* is to defeat the designs of the wicked.

10. *The Lord shall reign for ever.*—The eternity of the reign of God is contrasted with the brevity of man's (3, 4); and is a perpetual theme for praise, because it carries with it the blessedness of all souls and all worlds.

Psalm 147 "IT IS GOOD TO SING PRAISES!"

It is supposed that this Psalm dates from the re-establishment of Jerusalem (2), and the re-building of its walls (13). It might have been composed for the occasion mentioned in Neb. 12:27.

1. *Praise ye the Lord!* Heb. "Hallelujah!" *Praise ye Jah!*— The first verse is compiled from three other Psalms—92:1; 135:3; 33:1. The R.V. (*marg.*) suggests a beautiful alternative reading: "For He is good; sing praises unto our God, for His is gracious."

2. *The Lord doth build.*—Though Nehemiah and his companions wrought, yet they realized that the Lord was the true builder (Zech. 6:12; Matt. 16:18).

3, 4. *He healeth the broken in heart.*—Another of these marvellous contrasts. God of all the stars; yet healer of broken hearts, needing such gentle touches (Psa. 51:17; Isa. 57:15; 66:2). The Creator and Monarch is also Father. One "broken heart" is of more value than the stars. Bigness is not greatness.

6. *The Lord lifteth up the meek.*—What reversals are here! Hannah and Mary, and a host of saints have celebrated them in song (I Sam. 2:7, 8; Luke 1:48, 51-53). And in our Lord there is the most notable example of all (Acts 5:30, 31).

8. *Who covereth the heaven with clouds.*—To the devout heart there are no second causes; God is all, and in all (Psa. 104: 13, 14).

9. *He giveth to the beast his food.*—"Shall God give a ton of herrings to a whale for breakfast, and will He not care for me and my children?"

10. *He delighteth not in the strength of a horse.*—These clauses represent the *cavalry* and *infantry,* on which nations are accustomed to rely. God's deliverances are not given to these, but to those who trust Him utterly.

14. *He maketh peace.*—Here is the hope of distracted communities. God is the great Peacemaker (Job 34:29; Prov. 16:7).

15. *He speaks, . . . His word runneth.*—"He spake, and it was done" (Psa. 33:9).

16, 17. *He giveth snow.*—The snow is like wool, not only because it is white, but because it acts as a blanket; and, being a non-conductor, conserves the latent heat of the soil. The hoar frost resembles the fine grey ash of wood burned in the open air. *Who can stand before his cold?* Think of the retreat from Moscow!

18. *He . . . melteth them.*—"So it was on the day of Pentecost. The winter of spiritual captivity was thawed and dissolved by the soft breath of the Holy Ghost." And such gracious spring-tides come to us all by the direct and sovereign grace of God (Sol. Song 2:11, 12).

19, 20. *He showeth his words.*—We may plead for this—that He would manifest Himself and his Divine truth to us as He does not unto the world (John 14:22, 23).

Psalm 148 "PRAISE HIM, ALL HIS ANGELS!"

The universe is summoned to praise God. When Mr. Janeway was dying, he said: "Come, help me with praises!—yet all is too little. Come, help me, all ye mighty and glorious angels, who are so well skilled in the heavenly work of praise! Praise Him, all ye creatures upon earth! Let everything that hath being help me to praise God! Praise is now my work; and I shall be engaged in this sweet employ now and forever." Similarly in our loftiest hours we turn to these Psalms, and find that their expressions befit the tumultuous rush of our emotions.

1. *Praise ye the Lord!*—Gloria in excelsis!

2. *Praise Him, all his angels!* (Psa. 103:20, 21).—Not angels only, but all other created intelligences are to sound out Jehovah's praise.

3. *Praise Him, sun and moon!*—Here is the fabled music of the spheres.

4. *Praise Him, ye heavens! and ye waters!*—The very clouds, dark and sombre, or steeped in glory, praise Him. And all the immensities of space are vocal; so that, storey upon storey, the whole is one temple of unceasing adoration.

6. *He hath stablished!*—Two things are here: the permanence and the order of creation, which shall not be impaired, though the Lord shall make new heavens and new earth, any more than man loses his identity when passing through the dust of death. What a marvellous miracle is continually in process around us the renewal and maintenance of creation! And remember that all is directly due to our blessed Lord, to whom these praises are ascribed (Col. 1:15-19).

7. *Dragons, i.e.,* sea-monsters (R.V.*marg.*).

8. *Fire, and hail!*—The tempests which sweep our lives have, all of them, music in their hearts. There is a chord in the rush of every storm. Let us praise God in unison! All stormy winds only fulfil *His* command.

9. We speak of the silence of the hills. But they too have a voice; and every tree claps its hands, or sings in its myriad leaves (Psa. 95:4; Isa. 55:12).

10. *Beasts, and all cattle.*—The lowing of the cattle; the song of the birds; the hum of the insects—all are indispensable notes in the great hallelujah chorus.

11. *Kings and all peoples* (*see* Psa. 72:11; Prov. 8:15, 16).

12, 13. *Young men and maidens; old men and children.*—"The Psalms are Church songs, and all who from her congregations should join in them."

14. "*A people near unto Him.*"—"Far off . . . made nigh" (Eph. 2:13).

Psalm 149 SING A NEW SONG!

This Psalm, like the rest of these closing songs of Hallelujah, belongs to the days of Nehemiah and Ezra, when the long-restrained joy of the restored people broke into vigorous manifestation (Ezra 6:22). The praises of the "King" are, throughout, the theme and substance.

1. *In the congregation.*—We must not sing lonely songs. For this, if for no other purpose, we should frequent the meetings of God's people, to share the enkindlings of common worship.

2. *Let Israel rejoice! . . . let Zion be joyful!*—Our first creation and our second; our making and re-making; our natural and our supernatural life, with all that belongs to them of provision and nourishment—suggest themes of constant praise.

3. *Praise his name!*—The Kingship of Jesus is a matter not of terror, but of great and abounding joy. We never learn the secret of true gladness till Jesus holds court in our hearts; then the joy-bells ring, whilst the sounds of rejoicing are heard (Psa. 118:15).

4. *He will beautify the meek.*—It is a solemn question with which to close each day, "Art thou pleased with me, O blessed Master!" And this is the one prayer for every morning, "May I walk to-day so as to please God!" (John 8:29; Col. 1:10; Heb. 11:5).

5. *Let the saints be joyful!*—This may mean either that the saints already enjoy a foretaste of glory—or that they may be glad in anticpation of glory. But, though we devote our nights as

well as our days to it, we shall never reach the limits of praise. The nights of the exiles' grief are exchanged for nights of song (Job 35:10).

6. *In their mouth . . . in their hand.*—Whilst we praise God with our lips, let us never lay aside the sword, but imitate the servants of the good Nehemiah (Neh. 4:17, 18). Then the devil will be resisted, the flesh crucified, and the world vanquished, to the music of unceasing adoration (Eph. 6:17).

7. *To execute vengeance.*—Not their vengeance, but God's. But the Divine method of vengeance was also nobly illustrated in the sending of a Pentecost blessing on those who had been the murderers of the Lord (Acts 2:23-33).

8, 9. *To bind their kings.*—The law was very stringent in its denunciation of such as refused to acknowledge God (Deut. 7:2; 32:41). And there is coming a time when He shall put down all rule, and authority, and power; for He must reign (I Cor. 15:24, 25.) This Psalm may await the consummation described in Rev. 15:2, 3. Then we will sing it, as Isarel its song of deliverance on the shore of the Red Sea.

Psalm 150 "PRAISE GOD IN HIS SANCTUARY!"

The last Psalm is a tumultuous outburst of praise. The sea of adoration is swept by mighty tempests of feeling, which roll the billows forward to break in thunderous acclaim upon the shore. "The Psalms," says Dr. Chalmers, "have their final and most appropriate outgoing in praise—that highest of all the exercises of godliness." "As the life of the faithful," says Hengstenberg, "and the history of the Church, so also the Psalter, with all its cries from the depths, runs out in a Hallelujah." "There is nothing in the Psalter," says Dr. Alexander, "more majestic or more beautiful than this brief but most significant finale; as if in emblematical allusion to the triumph which awaits the Church and all its members, when through much tribulation they shall enter into rest."

"We have the place (1); the theme (2); the mode (3-5); and the universality (6)—of the praise to be presented to Jehovah. This Psalm is said by a Jewish tradition to have been sung by persons who came to present the first-fruits, while the Levites met them singing" (Psa. 30).

1. *In his Sanctuary.*—The sanctuary is the earthly temple; the firmament of his power the heavenly. Earth and heaven blend in common acts of praise. Every true act of worship on earth excites a response in yonder world—the home of praise.

2. *Praise Him for his mighty acts.*—For the enumeration of these, we should turn to such recitals as Psa. 105., 106, or to Col. 1:15-21.

3. *With trumpet, psaltery, and harp.*—We are not concerned as to the nature of these instruments. But let us remember that each of our emotions and faculties may be a musical instrument in the best sense. Praise Him with the sound of your love! Praise Him with hope and faith! Praise Him with meekness and patience! Praise Him with courage and strength! Praise Him in Christian work! Praise Him when tied by pain and weariness to a sick-bed!

6. *Let every thing . . . praise the Lord!*—Pull out the mighty stops in nature's organ!

> Let the bright Seraphim in burning row,
> Their loud uplifted angel-trumpets blow.

Let the gnat make music with the vibrations of its wings! Let every creature which is in heaven, and on earth, and under the earth, and such as are in the sea (Rev. 5:12, 13) be heard saying, "Blessing, and honor, and glory, and power, be unto Him that sitteth upon the throne, and unto the Lamb for ever and ever." Hallelujah! Amen.

INDEX

F.B. MEYER MEMORIAL LIBRARY

Devotional Commentary on Exodus

This descriptive, directive and devotional work will be a special help to the hungry soul, the busy pastor, the pressured evangelist, the weighted missionary, and the searching scholar. 476 pages.

Choice Notes on Joshua—2 Kings

F.B. Meyer designed the book to record understandable, accessable notes on the books of Joshua through 2 Kings. The reader will gain new insight and challenge for today from these Old Testament books. 208 pages.

Choice Notes on the Psalms

This chapter-by-chapter commentary examines the Psalms from three perspectives: the historical setting, featuring the inner struggle of David; the prophetical references to Christ; and the practical applications. 192 pages.

Devotional Commentary on Philippians

The compressed and profound teaching of Philippians is X-rayed in this verse-by-verse commentary. This popular devotional is characterized by loyalty to the Scriptures and applications to the needs of today's believer. 262 pages.